Embracing Eternity

The Life Force Does Not Die

Written and Illustrated by **Dr. Angela deAngelis**

Continuity of Life Series

Volume 1

Endings Are Beginnings:
Navigating Your Hard Times into Higher States

Volume 2

Embracing Eternity:
The Life Force Does Not Die

Volume 3

Transition and Survival Technologies:
Interdimensional Consciousness as Healing, Survival and Beyond

Volume 4

Healing Earth in All Her Dimensions:
Personal, Species and Planetary Healing Tools

Embracing Eternity

The Life Force Does Not Die

Written and Illustrated by
Dr. Angela deAngelis

Light Technology Publishing

ISBN 1-891824-67-8
EAN 978-1-891824-67-8

Published & Printed by

3 Light
Technology
PUBLISHING
www.lighttechnology.com

800-450-0985

PO Box 3540
Flagstaff, AZ 86003
publishing@lighttechnology.net

Contents

List of Figures

Author's Note

Thank you for visiting these pages. Our paths will touch awhile as this little book becomes a doorway into life, into each other and into our lives. Here the continuity of life grabs hold, makes its reality loud and clear. Here the life force makes its ongoing, ever-present streaming essence known.

This book, *Embracing Eternity: The Life Force Does Not Die*, is Volume Two of this four-volume *Continuity of Life* series. This second volume weaves a thread of essential understanding, building a necessary linkage between all life's challenges and physical deaths, and then extending that linkage to the life of the consciousness—well beyond what we may be limiting consciousness to. Much of the focus herein is upon the fundamental shifts, the LEAPs in awareness involved in mastering transition of any sort, including that of physical death.

We can consciously bring about effective shifts and transformations during each and every one of our transitions and deaths. We can engage in this process each step of the way, every day. It is all in how we live our lives—what we see and know while we live our lives. We can prepare for what may appear (from the standpoint offered by a physical lifetime) to be the ultimate death, physical death, and in this very preparation, realize that physical death is not an ultimate death but rather another step along the way, because . . .

THE LIFE FORCE DOES NOT DIE!

This knowledge is our birthright, and it is for us to use, to understand, to maximize and to carry with us into the next level of our existence as we survive. . . .

The Great Unfolding

By what truth,
do we see truth?

By what eye,
do we see
light speed?

By what touch,
do we see
walls dissolving
into space and time
beyond?

By what thread,
is woven
all we know
and
all we do not know
we know?

We are the never-ending stream
of all things healing,
transforming into life
from death. . . .
        THE LIFE FORCE DOES NOT DIE.

— Angela deAngelis

BASIC
LIGHT-ENERGY-ACTION-PROCESS
STEPS

LEAP Level	LEAP Type	Volume of *Continuity of Life* Series This Is Discussed In
Seeing Cycles	Ground Level of LEAPs	Volume One
One	Embracing	Volume Two
Two	Quickening	Volume Two
Three	Willing the Exit	Volume Two
Four	Leaping to the Next Dimension	Volume Three
Five	Ascending	Volume Three
Six	Catharting Beyond	Volume Three
Seven	Metascending to a New Niche	Volume Four
Eight	Achieving Metastasis and High Metaxis	Volume Four

Though I walk through the valley of the shadow of death, I will fear no evil.

PART I

DEATH AS A METAPHOR FOR HEALING

Part I of this book introduces the notion that death is not only cyclic but is ongoing all around us at all times. Accepting death as an eternal and integral part of life reshapes perceptions of endings and beginnings, transitions of all sorts, including physical death. Death itself is a healing, and death itself is a metaphor for healing. When we bring ourselves to consciously participate in all our transitions, the very meaning of death and transition expands well beyond material-plane boundaries. In fact, it becomes ever more apparent that any physical boundaries to our existences are essentially artificial, as existence is more than physical. Once the awareness of the vastness of our existences is exercised and thereby strengthened, we are imbued with powers to heal the fears, tensions, problems and obstacles that our previously perceived limitations may have generated.

Chapter 1

Learn How to Die

Wisdom is hidden in darkness. . . .
Know that only by striving
can light pour into thy brain.

—Thoth,

THE EMERALD TABLETS OF THOTH

Why learn how to undergo and navigate "in life" transitions and actual physical deaths? Why at this time? What are you telling yourself by choosing to read this? You are responding to your highest instincts. You are taking in a profound message, one that says:

"Honor your position on the precipice of time. Be alert. Stay very conscious. Learn the death technologies. You have the right to this knowledge, and you have the ability to learn it now. Make these precious moments in the time of your life matter. Move yourself from the role of what may seem to be a powerless pawn to that of potent player in the cosmic system by learning how to die consciously and ascend at will. Learn how to move in and out of your current "in life" situations, in and out of your physical reality, in and out of your body, in and out of light and the Light."

Start by learning that we live and die, we begin and end, we transition over and over, every single day. Participate fully in this never-ending stream of your existence to master deaths of every form. Always remember:

**THE LIFE FORCE DOES NOT DIE.
YOU DO NOT DIE.**

Keep Your Own Counsel

The way you live and the way you die matters. You are a participant in the massive escalation of both the speed of growing awareness and the speed at which some forces may seek to hinder this growing awareness. We are more easily controlled when we believe we die in the absolute sense. Once we fully see our *eternality*, our power reveals itself to us as ever more abundant. We become the dynamic expansive beings we are.

It is important to know this, to empower yourself with the tools this knowledge carries, in order to help bring about your rightful evolution. The forces of deception and truth, of enslavement and freedom, are intensifying their polarizations. Whenever polarizations are intensified to great extremes, the energy between the poles can arc, causing fleeting but deceptive flashes or switches in their charges. And so you must keep your own counsel, refine and mature your own counsel, to find your way through a maze of illusions in which even the darkest of forces can appear as pure, high or divine Light.

In this maze of emerging and competing realities and *irrealities*, including those concerning death, the markers on your path can be switched as if they were intersecting street signs being changed by devious pranksters. But this is not just about getting lost on a city street. The stakes are much higher in the maze of illusions. You can be led to believe you will cease to exist to such an extent that you convince yourself—on some very deep, unseen level—of the finality of your physical death. This surrendering of your innermost knowledge of who you are and what you are is not necessary and is really rather readily counteracted. Reawakening the consciousness (and fortifying the consciousness) is achieved by exercising it, a process these volumes guide readers into and through.

Look around. The zombification of humanity is well under way. Many people have been forced or brainwashed into abandoning themselves and most importantly their consciousnesses—surrendering their awarenesses of their eternalities. They walk, they talk, they feel, but they feel they do not live on past physical death. In this sense, they live this limitation in perception. "Living on" does not require a particular belief system, or a God, or even one's own physical body. "Living on" is something one's consciousness can choose to do. Yet more and more of us are being forced to conclude that the consciousness must die with the body.

You can help stop this sad trend. You can step into a more full relationship with your own consciousness. You can *know* whatever you need to know to feed your consciousness and to protect it. Whatever your stage of life or of so-called death, whatever your current level of transition, you can train yourself to consciously, at all times, map your territory. And you can learn well the difference between truth and deception, to effectively educate and apply your own counsel under pressure, even the pressures of intense living transition and profound physical death.

Navigate Acceleration

Times are changing ever more quickly. The opportunities for personal, species and planetary "quickening" are therefore greater than ever. The speeding up of change, this special degree of acceleration, can produce a profound and ecstatic LEAP (light-energy-action process) in awareness, a suddenly vaster multidimensional species intelligence and a rapid energetic connection or hook-up among beings. Yet the speeding up, especially when misunderstood, can also produce social, political, economic, ecological, emotional and spiritual disorganization and chaos. When resisted or mishandled, it can even produce massive convulsions—which, in the material plane, can take form as political upheaval, economic breakdown, mass hysteria, ecological disaster or cataclysmic shifts in the balance of the entire planet. However, more of this may be less necessary if we understand what is taking place on an energetic level before it physicalizes.

The dissolving and rerouting of previously locked-in and "stuck" energy systems, thought forms and ecosystems is necessary, although it does not have to be traumatic if we know how to navigate it and recognize the opportunity it brings. This rerouting of stuck energy systems allows for the release of trapped, stagnating or decaying energies. It also allows for the extensive restructuring of reality and allows movement among dimensions of reality. *Death is basically any movement from one dimension of reality to another, any major change.* This change or movement can be smooth, simple, even tranquil. However, it usually involves the decomposing and restructuring of patterns and energy matrices from one form to another. This reorganization of energy is always convulsive on some level, even when the level is subtle and relatively undetectable in the material realm. Yet the convulsion is simply a wave of transition into a more evolved state of existence.

Elect to Die Well

That you may at some point wish to die physically and/or in other ways, wish to be able to die and actually want to die well and with grace, will eventually become obvious to you. If you feel at all uncomfortable with the concept, understand that you are programmed to fear death and to justify this fear of death as a survival instinct. But this instinct was programmed (either by evolution or its engineers) right into your genes. You have a right to break free of this programming.

The simple and profound death and ascension technologies are your birthright. Knowing, practicing and applying these technologies is true survival. You will come to feel the difference between the so-called survival instinct that was programmed into you and your true desire to do what it takes to survive with whatever portion of your self, your consciousness, you wish to preserve. There can even be methods of reassembling what will seem to be your physical body or something very much like it after a physical death. You can and most likely will choose to learn these at some time during your existence. However, the greatest learning here is that your physical body is an expendable vehicle of your evolution. Eventually, it becomes unnecessary baggage. Experienced travelers learn not to overpack and not to overload themselves en route.

Learn to die well in order to make your death matter. Make every shift, change and challenge you face in daily life, practice for larger transitions and deaths. Learn about dying and how to die well while you are still living in your physical body so that you will understand the developments you face after you leave your body. The longer you have lived in your physical body— in the so-called material plane—the older you are in chronological Earth years, the more learning about dying there is for you to do. If you are still very young in Earth years, your natural response to death is as yet unfettered by the material-plane experience. You have not yet absorbed the overlay, taken on the veil that material reality renders.

The longer you live in the material plane, the more you must strive to know what is in this book. As you spend more years living in the material plane, what you instinctively know is buried more deeply and must be consciously relearned—you must *learn* to die well to be better at living and coping with life's challenges. You *learn to die* to understand that you can survive your physical death as well as any other challenging transition. You must learn and you most certainly can learn, no matter what your current condition.

Step back from yourself for a moment and see that you are part of several larger bodies. You are a cell within an organ of a living component of a larger living organism. The being you currently take form as exists and survives within your biological, ecological, cultural, economic, political, planetary, galactic and dimensional systems. Each of these interlinked systems now teeters on the brink of profound transformation. Should this transformation manifest as the transitional death of any or all of the systems in which you are a cell, it may take you through the process with it.

Learn how to die well and at will in order to navigate not only your own death, the death of your own physical system, but the transitional deaths of the systems in which you exist. You may at some point wish to divorce yourself from your own physical body or from the system in which you live to better survive. Learn to die, to divorce from your attachments to existing systems, in order to enhance your survival.

Break Free and LEAP

Without the death technologies and multidimensional shift concepts presented herein, you may feel like a prisoner in your physical body. You might feel to be trapped in physical (material) mortal reality. In this sense, you are incarcerated in your current incarnation. But this need not be your reality. You need not cease to exist along with any transitional or seemingly failing solar, ecological, economic, biological, cultural, occupational, family or marital system.

Tap into the light coming from higher dimensions of reality. Let it filter into your awareness. Take your power back by seeing what is actually here for you, by tapping into the inspiring and transformational and catalytic forces available to you. Fuel the LEAP in your awareness and in your energy structure that you must make in order to survive any so-called death. This *light-energy-action process* (the LEAP) is the key to survival during all transitions, transformations, transcendences—and deaths. This LEAP offers the key to transition.

The *death technologies* enabling this LEAP conflict with no belief system, religion or science on Earth (or in the cosmos). This is because these technologies can be taken in as concentration or meditation practices, as philosophical exercises, as science fiction games, as scientific explorations or as religious or transformational experiences. You decide, of your own free will, how you wish to absorb these death technologies. In the end, the choice between the mortality and immortality of your consciousness is yours. Learn to die and you will know this.

This book is a manual on and carefully presents the keys that unlock the LEAPs to transition, transformation and death. This volume guides readers through the progressive death awarenesses and related sequential LEAPs, each with their specific transition-death-ascension technologies. This is done by means of processes, exercises (numbered and in italics), contained in many of the chapters of this book. These exercises begin quite simply and carefully build toward some very esoteric understandings. These exercises are designed for use by most everyone, regardless of age, belief system, experience or health. Should any exercise require a physical activity (such as sitting, standing or reaching) that you find hard to do because you are physically weak, ill, incapacitated or perhaps being labeled "senile" or "comatose," just let yourself imagine that you are doing the exercise. Thinking through the motions described is tantamount to performing the motions when you do not have the actual option of literally doing them. Your mental circuitry is exercised either way.*

Whatever your level of physical and mental ability, your range of motion, your stage of life or your relative need for these

---

* Note that we include so-called "senile" and "comatose" persons in this list of those who may be unable to physically perform these exercises but can still benefit. This is because some spirits who seem to others to have no contact with material-plane reality linger, keeping the physical body alive, seeking support and guidance such as that transferred from between the lines of this book and from within these exercises in this book. This book can be read aloud to such beings. It is also recommended that pieces of this book be read aloud to those who have recently died physical deaths as guidance for the journey to come. Either way—as direction back to the physical plane or direction out and beyond—understanding navigation is highly valuable.

exercises, your spirit wants to enroll in this interdimensional travel school. To begin learning these transition and death technologies, spend a few moments conducting the following very basic exercises. Do these silently, in your mind. No writing is necessary at this point, although later exercises will suggest the use of pen and paper where possible. Again, for those unable or not wishing to use pen and paper, just imagine that you are doing so. There will come a time when you awaken outside your physical reality, when you will be glad that you have practiced thinking, even writing, in space and time without pen and paper. All participants in these exercises are asked to practice such thinking by conducting some basic exercises such as the following without doing any writing.

Exercise 1.1: Contacting Death Resistance

Think of three reasons—the first three that come to your mind—for you not wanting to die right now. Count these reasons as they come to you. If you do not have three reasons of your own, let some or all of your three reasons be those you think other people or society may have for you not to die right now. Your reasons can be of any nature, including fears, inconveniences, unfinished business and the leaving of loved ones behind.

Exercise 1.2: Contacting Release Resistance

Imagine that you have written each of these "three reasons not to die right now" down onto three separate pieces of paper. Now imagine the wind coming up and blowing away each of these reasons for you not dying right now. Do you feel anything about this imagined blowing away of your reasons not to die? Do you feel sadness? Or relief? Or surprise? To what degree do you feel any of these or other responses? If you feel nothing about this imaginary blowing away, ask yourself, how does "feeling nothing about the loss of reasons not to die" feel?

Note any resistance you felt to the idea of the wind blowing away your reasons not to die. Did you want to stop the event, as if saving precious papers from blowing off of a table? Relive each and every resistance to the blowing away of each reason not to die, whether subtle or distinct. Perhaps you felt nothing. Note any numbness or lack of response you may have to this exercise.

Exercise 1.3: Repeating Release

Repeat the above two exercises several times, trying on different sets of reasons not to die each time. Do no writing during this exercise or its repetitions. Think and visualize your way through these repetitions and examinations of your feelings, unaided by written notes.

You may wish to make notes on this exercise once it is completed. This is fine.

Stepping into greater sensitivity—a truly heightened sensitivity—to ourselves is part of increasing awareness of who we really are and part of enhancing our alertness to ourselves in all forms of transition. Again, transition is a perpetual state. Let's be aware of every step of the perpetual process and harvest great value from it. This is what learning to die is all about.

Chapter 2

Being Part of a Dying System

Many things indicate that we are going through a transitional period, when it seems that something is on the way out and something else is painfully being born. It is as if something were crumbling, decaying and exhausting itself, while something else, still indistinct, were arising from the rubble.

—Václav Havel,
"Philadelphia Liberty Medal Address"

Do you think about your death? Or do you avoid thinking about it? Does it seem to you to be a major event looming in your never-far-off future? Or does it seem so distant that it is irrelevant right now? When you cling to life, what are you hanging on to and why? Imagine what it feels like to have your body die.

Eco-Death

Would you know how to distinguish between signs of your own dying and signs that the system in which you live is dying?

Give some thought to this distinction. Certainly death is not an isolated event. It takes place amidst far larger events, far larger deaths, including the death of ecosystems.

We are seeing the emergence of *eco-death consciousness:* the awareness that transitional death is something happening to the larger systems in which we live. This is the time in modern history when we feel mounting *system pressure to evolve* (to change or die or both) as a social, economic and ecological species system. At least the signs are interpreted this way: we are surrounded by and living within economic, social and environmental systems in transitional states commonly described as decline. In this environment, death works its way into the corners of everyone's mind.

Many children, who might instead be playing house or tag but who sense at least vaguely that they may face a tenuous future in this precarious physical-plane world, have things to tell us about being part of a dying system:

> *"I think the Earth is dying because people litter and treat the Earth with no respect. The Earth is sick. All the big pollution makes the Earth have a high fever."*

> *"Animals can be harmed by plastics in the water, the pollution in the air. So, of course, kids can too. Isn't it obvious?"*

> *"In ten or fifteen years, we're all going to be freakin' dead, because everyone's polluting the Earth."*

Ask children and teenagers what it is like to be so young and worry about eco-death, to be thinking that the Earth's biosphere is overpolluted and maybe even in trouble: "How do you live knowing this?" They reply:

"I'm kind of ticked off. Really angry, actually."

"I worry quietly but act cool about it."

"I have bad dreams about it, but you have to just go on with your life."

"A lot of people will have to die before grownups fix things. It's just the way it is."

Species Death

If you tell children, "When I was your age, I didn't wake up in the middle of the night or in the morning with this sort of thing on my mind. I didn't think about things like pollution and dying very much back then," they seem to understand that times have changed. They seem to give voice to humans' growing sense that they may face the possibility of species death. As one child wonders:

"Sometimes I ask myself why we're actually alive. If the Earth is dying, you know we have to be dying too, don't we?"

Ask the children who talk with what seems to be such pessimism, "So what does it mean to be alive when the planet is dying?" They say:

"It's kind of scary. I mean, all of a sudden you could die

just because you're on this Earth. And if it's not pollution, it's maybe something else. All of a sudden we all can just go into a black hole and get dead!"

Ask them, "Are most young people scared these days?" Some say:

"Not all of them."

"Well, most kids are like the adults. They don't really care."

"Most kids don't care or don't know about this or just don't want to think about it because they're very, very scared."

"I think about it. I wake up in the morning and I think, 'Why the heck did I get born now? Why now? Why am I here? How am I living? What's going to happen if the planet goes down?' I think all these stupid questions to myself. I can't answer them, and it really bugs me."

Ask them, "Are you scared?" They reveal:

"Yes, of course, silly."

"No, not me."

"Well, I don't want to die by the time I'm twenty-five! I want us to be alive. I want us to die of being old and not

because the world is all junky. I don't want to think about dying for a long, long time, but I have to because of what is going on in the world."

Ask, "Do you mean that our ecosystem is sick?" "*Yes,*" some respond succinctly. Others' responses to this question are quite unusual:

"When the space people come here in the future, they're going to get sick on Earth like we did—I mean like we will, and are."

Some children say:

"A lot of people think it's God's fault, because He didn't teach us how to live here. But He created the trees and the plants, and He wanted us to treat the planet really good."

"Some people do treat Earth okay. In some countries, there is not one piece of trash. They really take care of their world. But here where I live, people just throw their cigarettes down and their trash down, and it really makes the Earth sick. And kids and other people are going to get thrown into the Sun or hit by a comet, because pretty soon everything is going to die and God can't pick up the trash."

Children who focus on the death of the planet may seem to tie littering in with ecological disaster and tie that in with cosmic destruction such as black hole swallowings. The logic may be confusing, but the sense that we are indeed part of a dying or at least transitional system is being expressed:

"So we're all going to die. That's why people don't care anymore."

Ask them, "Die? You say 'die.' What is death?"

"Well, there are a lot of ways you can die. It can be because of Earth and what happens to the Earth. It can be from drugs or cigarettes or AIDS or something like that. Or it could be something else—you know, like if you have breast implants, you can get sick too. Even a heart transplant can kill you to save your life."

Inquire, "So is that what makes you think of death? The dangers or risks of living?"

"Yup."

"And all the dying things around me."

Sometimes suicide works its way into the conversation:

"Death is when the world dies, when we all die, or when we all start taking drugs or something like that, trying to kill ourselves."

Ask, "Do some people kill themselves on purpose?"

"Yeah. Suicide is another thing that kills."

Ask, "What is suicide?" The answers vary:

"Suicide is when a person says, 'I don't want to live anymore.'"

"Say some person got mad and didn't want to live anymore. Say his life was miserable, so he kills himself. He shoves a knife through his heart or something. Maybe he kills himself by jumping off the Golden Gate Bridge or some other big bridge."

Note children's conversations about suicide:

"I heard on the news that a woman wanted to give her liver to her husband because he was dying."

"If she did such a thing, do you think that it was nice of her to give up her life for his?"

"Yeah, but she would probably say, when we get divorced, I'm taking the liver with me."

"You mean her kidney—didn't she give her kidney to her husband? Because she probably had two kidneys."

"Yeah, that's what it was. But that's almost suicide too. And also, I heard on the news that some people have a kid with a kidney problem. The kid is about to die because of a kidney problem, so the parents take their newer baby's kidney and put it in the sick kid. Well, this could kill the baby. What if the baby gets older and has a kidney problem too? Have another baby to get another kidney?"

Ask children what the question behind this sort of discussion is. After thinking for a while, they frequently reply:

"Well, I think the real question is who should live."

"Yeah, ha-ha, who should get to live here long enough to see the world die."

Are children who concern themselves with such matters fatalistic or realistic? Are they responding to a deep-seated awareness or to the sensationalism of the evening news? Or both? How much of what young people say displays for us some of our most silent thoughts?

Political-System Death

The sense that the large systems in which we live could be troubled and breaking down or in some sort of profound transition is not limited to children. Many adults share in some form the above ecological and cosmic (comet- and black-hole-type) concerns. Other adults turn this sense that overarching systems are collapsing—or at least shifting in major ways—to the political and economic systems in which they live.

This is not surprising. For many adults, political and economic systems are more "real" and more "relevant" than ecological and cosmic systems. We can learn a great deal about our responses to death by looking at the way we respond to changing or troubled political systems. The growing and no longer minority perception found in many political systems of the planet is that the systems are shaking, shifting, perhaps even wearing out—dissipating, weakening and becoming ever more vulnerable—and that perhaps modern governmental, economic and social systems have outlived their focuses, purposes and efficiency.

The sociopolitical structures that have been built in recent centuries can indeed look more and more like houses of cards, creaking in the wind. Winds of change are rattling institutions of tradition, eroding them to their conceptual, skeletal profiles. Up to a point, people struggle to preserve them. Eventually people give way to the winds of change. Eventually they let the structures fall.

Yes, we finally let the old structures fall. *We let the old structures of the reality we have constructed dissolve.* We reach a point where we can invest no more in the preservation of dying systems. We realize that our true survival actually depends upon our willingness to see beyond the reality we know, *to let the old reality die.* Cling to a sinking ship too long and you will drown.

One of the greatest stresses on political and economic systems around the world is the mounting competition among peoples. Inequity becomes more obvious, political debates more heated. We beat at each other for a way out of the confusion of this reality. Violence erupts and intensifies as the population of humans does not address the very deep programming and conditioning that is driving this violence.

Knocking on Heaven's Door

On a deep level, we are beating on the walls of the material plane. We suspect that physical death is the great equalizer. We are "knocking on heaven's door" (lyrics from a song that became popular in an "eve of destruction" era, the 1960s). Yet do we realize what it is that are we knocking on?

We let ourselves think we are knocking on the door to human rights or some other justice; however, we are pounding on a far more formidable wall. We are knocking on the door to the beyond, and there, justice and the fair distribution of opportunity is profoundly unclear when looking at it from here. It is doubtful that there is actually a single heaven or a single set of entrance criteria into the next world. Who gets in? Into what? Who has a right to be there? Be where? Who shall live past this physical life? Who has the right to decide this? Isn't this something we can all choose for ourselves?

Cultural conflicts offer great lessons! They teach us how desperate we are to distract ourselves from death and truth. We realize, on some level, that the superficial distinctions among members of the human race are shields. Of course, each of us is a particular gender and ethnicity. Of course, each of us is our own parents' descendant. Yes, we are all the sex/race/class/nationality/ideology identifications that we either chose willingly or surrendered to have imposed upon us.

But these shields are barriers. They are physical barriers made out of skin between us and our true selves. The problem of discovering who we really are, both as individuals and as life forms, is so much greater than is reflected by our current efforts to be represented within our chosen or appointed groups—so much bigger than those we dance out in the name of competition. This identity crisis belongs to all of humanity. And as its political systems are wearing out, are dying into transition, humanity is intensifying its identity crises.

Is all the noise made this side of death heard on the other

side, in another dimension? What is it that humans are trying to resolve as they pass through their earthly journeys? What is it that all their efforts to hammer out political rights and opportunities will achieve in the longest of long runs? Much (but certainly not all) of the noise made about problems on Earth, in the material plane, may be made to drown out far larger concerns about dying, to look away from death.

Death is an equal opportunity. No matter what your social status, the death of you in your current form is coming to you at some time. However, you need not die along with the dying systems in which you presently find yourself.

Exercise 2.1: Seeing the Dying System

You live within many different systems. Without writing, think of any systems in which you live—personal, physical, social, religious, political, economic, ecological—that appear to be having trouble these days. What about the difficulties they are having, if anything, suggests to you that the systems you have thought of may be winding down or at least in transition? Would you say that any of these systems are actually dying? Why?

What are the signs that a system is dying? Can people sense such a death, or need they be told how to see it? How do you sense such a death? Remember, there are no right or wrong answers to the questions asked in these exercises.

Exercise 2.2: Separating from a Troubled or Dying System

Select one of the troubled and/or dying systems you identified in the previous exercise. Close your eyes and see where you fit within, see yourself in this system. See how very much a part of this system you are. See how tied to it—even defined by it— you are. Do you have any day-to-day reality that is not defined by this system?

Now, with your eyes still closed, use your imagination to create a way for you to exit this system. See yourself exiting. Get all the way out.

How did you choose to get out of this troubled or dying system? Did you choose to physically die? Or did you choose to create or visualize a window and simply climb through it? Maybe you chose to speak out and try to change the system? Maybe you chose to pull off a great escape during which official members of the system attempted to hold you back? Did you die trying to get out? How do you know this? Did you survive your exit? How do you know this?

Try this exercise a few more times, each time selecting a different type and size of dying system. Note mentally (write later if you wish) your means of exit each time.

Ultimately, we are concurrently and perpetually living through our own processes as well as the many processes of the systems in which we live. Any sensation of beginning and ending, any awareness of our own transitional states, any death we undergo, is taking place within larger beginnings and endings, transitions and deaths. The matter becomes more one of choosing which, if not all, of the transitions we are moving through we want to hold in focus.

Chapter 3

Defining Death and Death Technology

State upon state is born,
covering upon covering
opens to consciousness of knowledge,
in the lap of its Mother the soul sees.
—"Nineteenth Hymn to Agni,"
Hymns of the Atris,
the Rig-Veda

You may not always find yourself—or feel yourself to be—suspended in air. It is therefore best to begin thinking of your air as *atmosphere* now, so that you can transfer what you are learning here into many different atmospheres, realities or dimensions of reality.

Reach out into the air (or atmosphere) in front of you. Pretend that you find a window in that atmosphere. Pretend that you open that window. What you believe you find coming in from beyond that window is determined by what you believe is there. If you are afraid of what you think is there or of what you don't know about what is there, you will find your fear flowing in.

Fear of death stems from fear of the unknown. Once you define death in a way with which you are comfortable, you need not fear your death. You can open the window of change and transformation with confidence and even joy. You can look forward to such openings. You can learn the means—the technology—of traveling through such openings with grace and power.

What Is Dying?

Dying is going through transition. Dying is shifting into a different dimension of reality. As explained at the beginning of chapter one of the previous volume, *Endings Are Beginnings*, there are many forms of death:

> This [material] is written for anyone who is undergoing, has undergone or will undergo a major ending or transition, or a death of any sort—which, of course, is everyone. This includes divorce, being fired, leaving home or having one's children leave home. It includes abrupt changes or endings, such as having one's home collapse in an earthquake, receiving a serious injury or having something precious stolen. It also includes gradual but definite changes, such as changes in behavioral patterns—shifting out of a steady or addictive relationship to a drug, a person or a behavior; outgrowing a stage of life, a philosophy, a religion or a cult; aging or having all one's oldest friends die; or undergoing the disease process, whether it is temporary, chronic or "terminal." And, of course, we include the concept of dying, with which we all think we are so familiar: physical death,

which is seen by many people as the ultimate form of death. Indeed, physical death—fear of it, avoidance of it, viewing it as final—is an excellent model for all the deaths, small and large, that each and every one of us endures.

Dying is basically opening to change, willingly or not, ready or not. Dying is reorganizing: moving energy around, rearranging it. That's it! Dying is upsetting (or even overhauling) the apple cart and at least redesigning the display of your fruit. Dying is picking up the dice, shaking them and then rolling them to yield a new number. Dying is stepping out of the game you have been playing.

You might be saying, "If dying were really this simple, there would not be so much trauma associated with it!" Yet there are many profound elements of this trauma. Among these elements are fear, pattern addiction, materialism and other problems of attachment. Several problems of attachment have been introduced in the previous volume, including fear, pattern addiction and addictive materialism. We will later return to these elements of *the great but needless fear of transitions and deaths*. For now, let's briefly examine the general nature of problems of attachment, for it is attachment that makes most dying difficult to do and all change, shifting, movement or expansion difficult to manage.

Why Attachment Is an Issue

How important is it to understand attachment? Very. Attachment is pervasive. For most of those who live in physical and emotional reality, forming and then dissolving attachment is the greatest challenge. We become attached to our realities: the way we organize and relate to our lives, our possessions, our time, our relationships, our feelings. We form obvious attachments and we form less-than-obvious, subtle, hidden attachments. When the time comes to change or move on or die, these attachments must be released. Like children clinging to baby blankets, we may fight this release.

Identify Your Web

We tend to resist the release of an attachment, even when we do not know that attachment exists or to what extent we have developed it. And we frequently resist this release of attachment without realizing we are doing this resisting.

We resist release because we confuse our *selves*—our *consciousnesses*—with our web of attachments. Releasing attachment therefore feels much like we are losing ourselves, losing everything we know ourselves to be, losing our identity, our meaning, even dying, when all we are really doing is releasing attachments.

We anchor ourselves so deeply in the web we create that *we think we are the web*. This confusion between the self and the web it generates is understandable. After all, selves and webs of attachment are both invisible to the eye. To truly *see* these subtle structures—the structures of selves and then the structures of attachments—and the very real difference between them takes concentration and training. This training is a basic key of the consciousness and death technology set forth in these volumes, and is essential in refining our awareness.

Let's begin this training here: You have a consciousness, you have a body, and you have a web of relationships to the world around you. Consult Figure 3.1. Think of your *body* as your *instrument* of operation. For many, this body is somewhat like a car—it is how you get around and do things here in the material plane. Think of your body-instrument as having a technician to operate it or an operator-musician to play it. This operator-musician is (for the most part, although some feel they are operated by consciousnesses outside their own) your *consciousness*. Think of your consciousness as being busy using (or allowing) the body-instrument to weave an intricate web made up of cords, or strings, or strands of energy, or light, or music.

The relationship between the instrument or vessel (your body), the consciousness (your core consciousness) and the web your consciousness weaves via your body, can be confusing, as these overlap. The boundaries between these three basic manifestations of you are often unclear from within these three overlapping but distinct pieces of you. Looking out from within your body-instrument, through your web of attachments, the vision of your consciousness may be clouded. Be patient with your understandings of these three pieces: consciousness, body, web of attachments. The distinction becomes more clear as you think in terms of the reality of this distinction:

your consciousness →
(flows through) your instrument (your body) →
(to weave) your web of attachments

YOU ARE NOT YOUR BODY.

YOU ARE NOT YOUR WEB.

YET YOU ARE ATTACHED TO THESE.

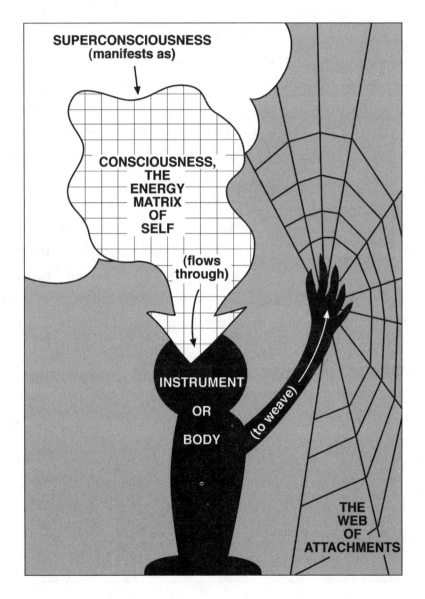

Figure 3.1. Oh, the web we weave.

Also note that:

YOUR LIFE FORCE IS NOT YOUR PHYSICAL BODY.

YOUR LIFE FORCE IS NOT YOUR WEB OF ATTACHMENTS.

YOUR LIFE FORCE DOES NOT DIE WITH YOUR PHYSICAL BODY.

YOUR LIFE FORCE DOES NOT DIE WHEN YOU RELEASE ATTACHMENTS, WHEN YOU STEP OUT OF YOUR WEB.

YOUR LIFE FORCE DOES NOT DIE.

Examine Figure 3.1 again. Note that Figure 3.1 suggests that some form of greater or superconsciousness generates your consciousness. Also note that, as indicated in Figure 3.1, your consciousness generates a very fine energy structure, or *consciousness matrix*. Your physical body can be seen as a manifestation generated by your consciousness matrix, as is the web of attachments you weave in your physical lifetime through your body.

Take these concepts into your mind slowly. Your physical body does not actually do all the weaving, as fingers of emotions are embedded in many attachments. But your physical body establishes your physical presence in physical reality and enables you to form physical and emotional relationships and their attachments to physical beings and objects, even ideas.

A human living in physical reality tends to confuse his or her consciousness matrix with its manifestations. These manifestations include the physical body and emotional, economic and other attachments, as well as awareness of the consciousness itself. This is one reason death frightens many physical humans. The human is afraid to lose him- or herself when faced with death. He or she assumes that the consciousness lives in and only in the physical body.

However, one's body is merely one's house, not its resident. Actually, it is the very fine structure we can call the consciousness matrix—which is not the consciousness itself—that is actually going to have to transform and which *can indeed* transform. What feels to be death beyond physical death—the death of the consciousness, of the self—is actually both:

(1) the shedding of the *manifestations of the consciousness matrix* (the shedding of the body and the web it has woven)

(2) the reformatting of the *consciousness matrix*, but not the losing of the *consciousness*

Exercise 3.1: Distinguishing the Instrument from Its Music

Imagine a symphony performing a concert. Musicians (consciousnesses) perform using instruments (musical vessels or bodies). A web of notes is formed. This web, once connected to ears, appears to be music. The musical web flows into the air or atmosphere from the instruments. The musicians, using their instruments, weave the web of sound in such a way that a concert is released into the atmosphere. They weave a specific collection of sounds. These sounds or energies flow as long as the musicians continue to produce them.

Become one of the musicians for a moment. Play the music. Imagine you see the web of sound you are producing. Hold on to this image. Play on. See the web become more elaborate. Distinguish between the musicians, including yourself, and the music they and you are playing. Stop all playing. Note that when you all cease playing, the physical sound web disappears or appears to disappear. See (or hear) the web disappear. It may appear to fade away slowly the way some sounds seem to do, or it might seem to stop being a sound immediately.

During this lifetime of yours, you weave a concert or web of attachments. When you stop weaving or playing your music, when you pack up your instrument and go home to another reality, the concert you wove spreads out like ripples on a lake. Similarly, when your physical body dies, the web your physical body wove for you appears to fade. Know that you are neither your physical body nor the web you have woven. You yourself fade away only if you choose to. *When you go through a major transition in life or a physical death, you—the ultimate essence of you, what becomes of your unattached consciousness—does not fade along with its fading physical body or its webs. Your consciousness matrix may or may not fade entirely. In fact, you can consciously choose to maintain your consciousness matrix, or let some of it go, or release it all.* The advantages of understanding the issues involved in releasing your consciousness matrix will be made clear in Volume Three.

You must fully release the physical body and the webs you have woven via this body's presence to focus on the survival and transformation of your consciousness matrix. Let go to live. Let go of what you have been led to believe you are; let go to allow what you truly are to live. The choice is yours, so long as you know that you can make it. So practice making this choice. Making this choice is the real dying, a very conscious dying that can be conducted while physically alive to stay physically alive, or that can be conducted during a physical death. Learning this is the next step in our evolution as individuals and as a species.

Exercise 3.2: Separating Yourself from Your Web

Close your eyes. Now imagine yourself to be a musician. Play the instrument of your choice. Play a brief note.

> *Now, with your voice, make an actual (audible) sound, repre-senting that note. Sing or tone or hum or make a one-vowel sound such as "oooo." As soon as you play the note, say goodbye to it.*
>
> *Do this several times, as if you are blowing bubbles, as if each note you make is a bubble. You know the bubble will soon pop, so you say goodbye to it, detach from it, immediately after blowing it. Play a note. Say goodbye to it. Play another note. Say goodbye to it. Continue this way for a while. . . .*

Again, when you go through a major transition in life or a physical death, you can mistakenly identify with and hang onto the web—what you hear as being the concert of notes you have created. This is like hanging onto a disintegrating or sinking ship. It's going down—why stay there? Do not confuse your web or the things, bodies, events to which you attach your web. Do not confuse your physical body, your physical instrument, with your self. It is easy to confuse these things; however, survival requires knowing the difference.

Your body and the web it weaves is your temporary address, part of an ever-changing map. Maps change. Maps come and go. However, *you* do not necessarily come and go. The survival of your consciousness is up to you.

Consciousness Matrix

Your consciousness creates your consciousness matrix. Even that matrix is a step removed from your consciousness. However, the consciousness matrix is much closer to your consciousness than the web you weave or the physical body you grow. Both your consciousness (who you are) and its consciousness matrix (what who you are forms itself as being) will last as long as you choose to maintain them. These can be nonphysical components of your self.

> consciousness ➤ consciousness matrix ➤ web ➤ physical body

Sovereignty

You are the territory; you are not the map. You are not your body, not your web. Yet it is easy to confuse *your attachment to the map of your territory* with your territory. The map is too often better tended than the territory. The maintenance and cultivation of the territory itself is neglected. The consciousness starves for nourishment.

Over time, after your (even unintentional) prolonged neglect of your consciousness, your sovereignty (your free will) is compromised, surrendered by this neglect. Of course, this neglect is largely unintentional and unconsciously conducted, and is more the product of material-plane distraction and coding to be distracted by the material plane. (We have to think about what drives this unconsciousness neglect and whether individuals are entirely responsible for this tendency. What other factors or forces may have an investment in the disempowering of individuals' free wills?)

Sovereignty—what is sovereignty? Sovereignty is self-rule. You are the sovereign, the ruler, the queen or king of your consciousness and its matrix. You are in charge of your kingdom of consciousness so long as you choose to be. Do not take major changes in life and physical death as pressure to relinquish sovereignty.

Do not misinterpret the message here. You have full right to yield control of your consciousness, to merge your kingdom with another consciousness (perhaps one that is more divine, more powerful, or more benign, or more seductive). Yet you have full responsibility to know that you are doing so and to know to what or whom you are relinquishing the precious energy of your consciousness. To whom are you surrendering your right of self-determination and your energy?

There is great temptation during death and any profound transition to surrender the self without a careful examination of the power to which you are surrendering. Remember that profound transition and even physical death do not result in the killing of your free will. On the contrary, *your transitioning and dying is, when consciously conducted, the raising of the power of your free will!*

Exercise 3.3: Opening the Window

This is an incredibly simple foundation exercise, designed to initiate the expansion of your understanding of death. Regardless of its simplicity, conduct the exercise as described.

Imagine that you are in a dark room. It is night. You are facing a closed window. It is bolted shut. Reach out with your hands. Unbolt this imaginary window, and open it.

Let the moonlight, the starlight and any kind of celestial light you can imagine pour in through the open window. The light showers you and fills you. With your eyes still closed, hang on to this image as long as you can. Move into the next exercise with it.

Exercise 3.4: Moving Through the Window

Move now, by moving your arms as if you are swimming, through this open window. Swim toward the source of the light that is filling you. Move into the next exercise as you swim toward the source of light that is filling you.

Exercise 3.5: Basic Reformatting

As you fill with light, notice that, feel that, imagine that you change from a physical body, made up of flesh and bones and organs and blood, to an increasingly lighter body, made up of less and less of what you think of as your body. Think about how every cell of yourself is turning into a new substance (or nonsubstance, for that matter). Try to get detailed as you visualize this simple reformatting, reconstituting.

Read on patiently and with focus. You are now on your way into the basic reorganization of your awareness required to assimilate death technology.

Chapter 4

Accepting Death and Understanding Grieving

He holds nothing back from life;
therefore he is ready for death,
as a man is ready for sleep
after a good day's work.

—Lao Tzu,
Tao Te Ching

If you ask young people, "What happens when you die?" they reply:

> "When you die, you go into a coffin and you get buried under the ground. And then there are angels, and they come and take you up there, and you either become an angel or you go to hell."

If you ask, "What is hell?"

"It is where everything is bad and hot. It's all fiery and steamy. Some people think there is the devil there."

If you ask, "What is a devil?"

"The devil is like a bad man in red."

If you inquire, "Do you believe in the devil?"

"No, but I believe that if you believe in him, you find him."

If you ask, "What do you believe happens when you die?"

"If you're good, you go to heaven."

"And where do you go if you are not good?"

"To hell."

If you inquire, "You believe in hell but not the devil?"

"Well, there might be a devil; he runs the place. You go if you're bad."

"Oh."

"There is no such thing as hell. I mean, hell is used in sayings like, 'What the hell?' But there is no such thing as hell, that's what I think. When you die, you either get cremated or you get put in a coffin or your body gets floated out to sea or

something. Your spirit just goes on. When it finds something
it wants to be in your next life, you will be another thing."

Fear of Death

When you die, you will become, transform to another energy matrix, some other form or format of energy. Are you afraid of taking on a new form? This fear need not burden you; this fear need not arise.

Many persons are afraid of death. Many persons are beyond afraid—they are terrified. Although they may not let on, their terror in the face of death is almost indescribable in words. Many a person confronts the unknown future, the death, wailing silently into the void, screaming inwardly. A continuous but silent scream rings throughout them. Many a soul refuses to let this fear energy out. Many a soul in-presses this fear inward instead of outwardly expressing it. It is important to allow the outward expression of fear so as not to trap the fear, not to cage it, not to keep it inside, not to have it fester there and not to have it take over.

Fear takes energy from you when you keep it trapped inside you. Fear takes you from you. Immersed in unreleased fear, you lose yourself. When you can release your fear, you can decide for yourself how much emotional and physical suffering you choose to undergo in any of your dyings, physical or otherwise.

Exercise 4.1: Expressing Fear

Stand with your eyes closed. Imagine that you stand before a closed door. You are about to beat at this door to the unknown, as if you want to see what is behind it. Do not beat at this door because you want to go beyond it, to be what you call dead. Beat because you want to know what awaits you.

Now you raise your hands in front of you. Clench each hand into a tight fist. Beat silently against the invisible door or wall that stands before you. Keep those fists clenched very tightly. Beat silently, at first slowly and then more and more rapidly. Beat harder now.

While you are beating, imagine (but do not make any noise) that you are screaming into each of those beats. Just imagine this. Make no audible noise.

Now imagine, in silence, that these screams are becoming deafeningly loud. Imagine that you are attempting to keep these silent screams within your mouth. You are refusing to let the screams out. Clench your lips so that your screams cannot get out while you continue to beat at that door so very fiercely, so very desperately. That screaming is pressing to break through your lips.

Suddenly, the silent screaming breaks through your lips and you actually scream out loud! Scream! Make noise! Scream louder! Scream longer! Imagine that you are never going to stop this loud screaming. Mix in some wailing with your screams. Wail! Wail! Waaaaa! Now your despair is breaking through into the sound of your screams and wails. Keep screaming. Hear yourself screaming.

Now stop beating on the door. Stop screaming. Take a deep breath, hold it a moment, and then release it very slowly. Hold this position for the next exercise.

Exercise 4.2: Releasing the Last Fear

In complete silence, close your eyes and examine your inside. Are you in physical or emotional pain? Are you tired? Are you tense? Are you sad? Are you empty? Move your attention slowly from the top of your head downward throughout your body. Is there a scream left anywhere in there?

Find a remaining scream or a point of unexpressed fear, sorrow, *pain or tension within you. Without making a sound, go back into this scream. Hear it silently sounding itself. Scream silently. Make no audible noise yet. Raise your fists and bang on an invisible door. Force yourself to bang harder now. Harder! Even if you do not feel you need to bang harder, do so. Exaggerate your pounding. Even if you do not believe there is even a tiny scream left, repeat the above Exercise 4.1 as follows:*

Force yourself to scream and wail (aloud if you can) until you are absolutely certain that you have exhausted the screams for now, until there is nothing left, no unreleased pain, no unreleased anxiety, no unreleased fear. Scream and wail and flail your arms, maybe even stomp your feet until you have released all you can find to release.

Hold for the next exercise.

Exercise 4.3: Filling with Acceptance

If you feel you have fully released during the above exercise, you will feel relatively empty inside. With your eyes closed, see yourself as an empty vessel. Decide that you will fill that vessel with a specific feeling: a very pure acceptance. This pure acceptance is calming, soothing, reassuring. Give this acceptance a fluid image. Let it pour through you slowly, gently, quietly. Try to purify, to clarify this sense of acceptance by concentrating on it, getting to know it very well. As you familiarize yourself with the feeling of acceptance, tell yourself what it is you can have yourself do later, in the near and far future, to remind yourself of how acceptance feels.

Accept Grief as Grief for Your Attachment

Loss of a loved one tends to bring on a strong but vague sort of bewilderment, estrangement or just plain sadness. Some persons experience this loss more visibly than others; however, the loss or the effect of major change is there. If you have ever "lost" some-one—and we will call it "lost" for now—you know about grieving.

Keep in mind that the grieving process is most valuable when you, the grieving person, assume the perspective that the death being grieved is your own rather than that of a person you were close to. *What has died is the form—the material-plane, in-the-flesh form—of interpersonal relationship that* you *had with the deceased.* This relationship—especially if long-lasting in years, genetical-ly close or emotionally intense—has most likely generated a potent piece of web (an energy structure, or string) between you and the person you have "lost."

When a person who is one of the players in and also a com-ponent of an interpersonal energy structure dies a physical death, the physically attached elements of the interpersonal energy structure are destabilized. Imagine a molecule losing one of its atoms. Sometimes this molecule remains unstable for quite a while. Whether or not it is unstable, or measurably unstable, this molecule is no longer the same molecule.

Relationships—marriages, affairs, good friendships, family ties, many workplace relationships, even enemy relationships—are similar to molecules, with each person being one of the atoms. The way atoms are collected and held together in a mol-ecule is by means of electrical bonds. Energy, in the form of electrons, is shared among molecules. An energy web is formed. Strings, cords or bonds between atoms (members of the molecule) take on characteristics, vibrational patterns, frequencies of their own. If you remove an atom from the molecule, these bonds shift frequency, adjust, change in some other way or break.

Sometimes an individual who has lost a loved one claims

that although the loved one has died a physical death, that loved one has not broken all of the energetic bonds or dissolved the entire web built during the physical lifetime he or she has just departed. Some claim to communicate with "the dead," to maintain old bonds. Whatever your beliefs regarding communication with what you may describe as "the dead," know that *any communication or energy coming to you from outside the material plane is constitutionally different from the energy coming to you from within the material plane.*

Think about the transmission of energy in the form of sound between two material-plane atmospheres you know well: air and water. What do you hear of sound made in the air when you sit entirely submerged on the bottom of a swimming pool? If you sit outside a swimming pool, what do you hear when the underwater swimmer hums loudly?

If there is any communication or energy coming to you from loved ones who are what is commonly called "deceased," any message coming to you from the beyond (from what is beyond the material plane) will be different enough from what it had been before that physical death that you will not recognize it, or you will recognize it and immediately turn it into something that fits your reality, or you will somehow recognize it for what it is, finding that it is markedly transformed from its previous in-the-flesh originated signals.

You may try to hang on to the old physical-plane bond you had built with that person. You might even convince yourself that you are indeed hanging on. Still, something has changed. That being, if still conscious and in communication with you, is now in a completely different dimensional atmosphere. This means that the energy structure of your relationship is radically transformed. The strings or cords of the piece of web you shared are constitutionally different. There has been a great transformation at one end of the cord. When you die your next physical death, you will notice how incredible this transformation is.

When you hang on to an energy structure that is no longer formatted the way it once was, you are tying yourself—and sometimes tying the energy of the deceased being—to an illusion, an illusory notion of what that individual's energy form has become. Here is where you trap yourself—and sometimes your deceased loved one—in the shadow of a broken molecule. This is a dangerous trap. You tie yourself and your deceased loved one to an energy sink, a trap that consumes disorganized energy. The illusion that the old bond or old piece of web exists, that there is still accessible energy there in that old set of cords, can consume its participants.

The "dead" can be weighed down as they move on with their journeys and into new energy matrices they must form to fully transition. (Selection of what elements of new matrices will resemble or parallel those of matrices being left is best done by the person in transition, not by those who have not joined in that transition.) The "living" can be prevented from moving on with their lives. Of course, the terms "dead" and "living" are merely words for states of existence, with "existence" being the operational word here.

This condition is apparent among those who are undergoing long-term grieving processes regarding the loss of a loved one to physical death; of a spouse or lover to divorce or another relationship or event; of self-identity due to aging, illness or the end of a long professional life; or many other major life changes.

Exercise 4.4: Expressing Grief

Repeat the three exercises described above (Exercises 4.1, 4.2 and 4.3), this time with the sense that the object of your grief (usually a loved one) waits beyond the door upon which you are asked to beat in Exercise 4.1. When you start to scream and wail in Exercise 4.3, include the name of whoever (or whatever) you are grieving. Reach for that person or thing. Reach out as far as you can and cry out the name. Beg for the person or thing to return to you. Imagine that you have tied one or more ropes or cords to that person or thing, and tug on these cords. Pull on them. Freeze. Hold for the next exercise.

Exercise 4.5: Cord-Cutting Ceremony

Visualize the person or thing you have been tugging on. Imagine that this person or thing is speaking these words to you: "Release me. Cut the cords so that I may move on with your blessing." Respond, "I release you. I cut these cords so that you may move on with my blessing." Use your fingers as if they were scissors, and imagine that you are cutting a web of strings that once tied you to this person or thing.

Now see whoever or whatever you have just released turn to light and float a distance away . . . away, away, away, but not entirely gone from the cords of attachment that may be hindering this transition.

Feel only love, relief and acceptance. Work to clarify and to focus on these feelings.

Accepting death involves mastery of grief. Grief is a normal human emotion. Appreciate its richness and depth. Understand how real the experience of grief is for your emotional body. Experience grief. Taste it. Know it. And then expand beyond it.

Chapter 5

Preparing for Death—
Your Own and Others'

The last thought and emotion that we have before we die has an extremely powerful determining effect on our immediate future. . . . That last thought or emotion we have can be magnified out of all proportion and flood out our whole perception.

—Sogyal Rinpoche,
THE TIBETAN BOOK OF LIVING AND DYING

"But it's not fair! I'm not ready to die!" This anguishing lament is cried so many times! This fierce pain is associated with the human condition. Many will feel they are never ready. Even on their deathbeds, many struggle and fight the fantastic transformation they are about to undergo. They resist the magnificent understandings that would allow them to die with grace and power. How unfortunate, yet how very understandable. Assistance with knowing what death really means and is has not been available—and in fact, may have actually been repressed.

One must always be ready to die. This readiness is not suicidal. There is a big difference between being consciously ready to die and being hysterically on the brink of killing oneself. Conscious death at the right time is healthy. Hysterical death is not healthy; it is wasteful, destructive and dangerous. Conscious preparation for death prevents hysterical death. Three very important parts of preparing for your death (for any living death and for any physical death) are:

- the feeling of readiness
- the practical preparation
- the sense of closure

The following discussion applies also to preparing for the death of a loved one in two ways. First, you can help a loved one prepare for death when you understand how to prepare for your own death. Second, you can share the *sense of being prepared* for death with a loved one by *feeling prepared* for your own death. Moreover, everyone's life is filled with minor and major transitions. The best approach to preparing for death is to recognize that the death and transition path is walked perhaps millions of times in a lifetime.

Readiness for Death

Readiness for death is a healthy state of mind. Readiness implies that you are prepared, like an actor waiting for her or his cue, like a fireman or firewoman ready in case there is an alarm, like a lifeguard ready to leap into the pool should a child be at risk of drowning. The most prepared actors, firefighters and lifeguards do not sit nervously, waiting to be called. They are well trained; they know their lines, their procedures, their methods—their jobs. If you have ever studied for tests, you know how differently you feel when you have studied very well. You can enter the test with a high degree of confidence that most, if not all, of what you'll be asked to do will be something with which you are familiar, or something that you can figure out because you have dealt with similar challenges before.

So get ready for death! Know that the best way to live life ready for death is to deeply understand that:

- Every moment in the time of your life matters.
- The future is not entirely predictable.
- You must always be ready—ready for things to stay the same and ready for everything to change.
- You are already ready for your death: you have already explored the dying process, you already understand what dying is about, and you have already prepared yourself for your next dying. Now you must remember what you know.
- You can learn to die each and every time you undergo a change, transition, ending and then beginning.

Exercise 5.1: Being Ready for Death
Slowly read the above list aloud ten times. Read it as if you are telling someone else how simple it is to know these things.

Practical Preparation

Practical preparation for any major transition eases the passage. You already know this. Although it is not always possible to plan ahead for all life-changing and life-ending events, many persons can allow themselves the opportunity to "take care of business" by truly recognizing that we all undergo changes and transitions in life and we all eventually undergo physical death. Life is great training for death and vice versa. We are in transition every day, every hour, every minute, every moment. We live and die every time we change a little or a lot. We know death; we know life.

Planning around one's own physical death can be a good discipline for planning for other seemingly simpler transitions. It is not the goal of this volume to explore the legalities of various aspects of physical death. Readers are, however, encouraged to explore the following and related topics as far in advance of their deaths as possible:

- estate transmission
- the living will
- the storage or disposal of your own physical body
- the opportunity to specify the way you want to die

Generate Closure

Everything closes. Every day closes. Closing is natural. However, we overlook most closures in our haste and greed to live. One of the basic keys in the mastery of physical death is held in the hands of closure. Closure has a feel to it, a precious nature that can be enhanced when a closure of any sort is handled with awareness.

To generate closure, wake up each day ready for the day. Go to sleep each night acknowledging to yourself that you have completed that day. Review the day before falling asleep. Feel complete. Feel as if you have just read the last page of an immensely interesting book and that you are now closing the book and placing it on a shelf.

Do this review at the close of days, weeks, months, years. Even if you have what you call a "bad day" or a "horrible week" or a "losing season," be satisfied with the idea that you are living out a cycle and a cycle within a cycle. Observe as many cyclical endings and beginnings as you can, simply by acknowledging that they have occurred. Complete each day, week, month and year—each time cycle of your life—this way. Some of your observations will be quiet statements to yourself. Others will be celebrations with other people. Generate repeating closures.

Exercise 5.2: Practicing Cycle Sensitivity

Choose a recent time cycle of your life. You may pick the past hour, or the past twenty-four hours, or the past week, or the past season, or the past year, or the past decade. Think to yourself when it was that this cycle began and when it was that this cycle ended. As you are thinking, realize that this cycle is a cycle within a larger cycle, as are all cycles. Mentally review all the cycles that the cycle you chose fits into. For example, in terms of Western Earth time, a second is part of a minute, a day is part of a week and a century is part of a millennium.

Exercise 5.3: Studying a Cycle

Return to the cycle you chose in the above exercise. Think about what you might call the beginning of that cycle. Try to recall some characteristics you can associate with the beginning of this cycle: how you felt, how you looked, what was going on in your life or in the world around you.

Now pick out events during the middle of this cycle. Do not trouble yourself with efforts to put these events in order, in linear time sequence. Keep in mind that linear time is an illusion. It is a handy map for those who live in material reality, but it is only a map, not the reality. Allow the events that took place during your chosen cycle to come back to you in any order.

Now pick an event or series of events that you associate with the end of this time period. Think about these. See them as cycle completion points. Then also see them as re-cycle points, or cycle initiation points.

You have just reviewed a cycle of your life. Treat that cycle like a book that you can put on your shelf for safekeeping and take down and re-read anytime you like. Treat that cycle, that book, as a part of a series, a sequence, a chain of books. As you do, know that each whole book is also a chapter in a much larger book. You may or may not have the larger book handy. You may or may not yet have room on your shelf for the larger book. You may or may not know what the larger book is about. This not knowing is all right. One of the greatest adventures in death is the close of a cycle, with another perhaps yet unseen cycle emerging. Closures frequently feel like dyings. But the larger story can only come to you as you read on.

Exercise 5.4: Seeing Your Life Cycle

Imagine that your life has just ended at exactly this point in time. Briefly review your life. Try to group events, memories, that come to your mind in terms of whether they fit into the beginning phase, the middle phase or this (would-be) end phase.

At first, the memories may come to you in a jumble, with all the phases mixed together. To help feel that you are organizing your thoughts here, break your life into the three parts: beginning, middle and end. Use any sort of category of three that you want to. For example, divide up your life by years, or by relationships, or by health patterns. Now review the beginning phase. (Do not try to time sequence your *memories in great detail.) Now review the middle phase. Now the end phase. Spend several minutes on the last bits of this end phase. Breathe a sigh of relief when you complete this review.*

Remember that although closure is the end of a cycle, it is also a transition, even a transformation, into a new cycle. A constructive sense of closure—in fact, any sense of closure—does not come automatically. It is important to admit to what obstructs closure, to explain to yourself how you may be resisting closure, whether it be closure of a relationship, a career, an addiction, a phase or a particular physical existence. This requires a willingness to conduct an honest inventory of your life and the patterns within it. (Note that closure does not necessarily mean a complete and absolute shutting of the door on every element of a situation. It does mean selectively and with clarity seeing what, if any, components of the past you can pull forward, or may actually require pulling forward to transform to a new energy matrix.)

No matter how much you appreciate the cyclical nature of life, you may find that the close of a life cycle leaves you with the nostalgic or uncomfortable or maybe even desperate sense that you are unfinished. Think back: Have you ever felt unfinished, "left hanging," wanting more of something with none of it seeming to come? Have you ever seen a child resist leaving the movie theater when the movie ended, wanting more of the story? The logic of the story ending may have been obvious to a more experienced movie viewer such as the parent, but not to the child. Could you be this child in some way? Could chapters of your life, or your entire life, be this movie?

Exercise 5.5: Defining the Unfinished

Now that you have given some thought to the sensation of being unfinished, let's work with this idea. (You can use pencil and paper for this exercise.)

Make a list of everything you have not done that you would like to finish were you moving out of your city or town today. Title this list "Moving Away Today." Try to put at least five things on this list. You may have many, many more than five things on your list—this is fine.

When you have completed the list of what you would do were you moving away today, write a new list: list everything that you have not done that you would like to have done or to complete doing, were you being forced more urgently and more abruptly to depart. Label this new list "Forced Urgently to Depart." For this list, imagine now that you are being forced by the law, or by a political event, or by some kind of major change in the world, to leave your home and family, whoever that might be: parents, siblings, spouse, children or other very close kin or friends you have. Imagine you are being forced to leave them for good and will not be able to communicate with them again by telephone, mail or any sort of clear method you have used to date to communicate clearly with them.

Is this list different from the first one, the list you made when you imagined you were moving out of town with a less serious reason? What is it that you have not said or done given this more pressing reality?

When you have finished this second list, write a third. Say that your life is over—this life, the life you are in right now—tonight at midnight. Label this list "Die Tonight." What is it that you would do or immediately complete if you only had a certain number of hours left to live? How many things on the above two lists would you include? How many of those things would you discard as being not important given the short amount of time to live? What new things *would you include on this new list? Write this list, circling the new items, if any—items that come to mind when you are asked to imagine that your physical death is imminent.*

Now try to organize each of the above lists into categories—in terms of personal relations, money matters, work, commitments or other categories you think of.

Look slowly at each of your lists. Notice your reaction or absence of reaction to each item on each list. Put a little star next to the items that you feel you have some kind of emotional connection to—some kind of emotional feeling that says you really need to complete this item. Star items that elicit a feeling in the heart or the gut. This sort of emotion indicates that you would very much like to take care of these things before dying. Realize that you are in need of settling the feelings about these items, not necessarily these items. These feelings are the most unfinished of all items, not because they have to do with any thing or any person in particular, but because you are most emotionally attached to their process, completion or resolution. For the time being, it is enough to recognize that such attachments make it difficult to die with grace and power.

We will return to this matter in Part III of this book, where the question of how to detach is discussed.

Chapter 6

Spotting the Right Time to Die

When the last Lacandon dies, the world will come to an end.
—Chan K'in Viejo,
Lacandon elder and prophet,
as told to Victor Perera in
THE LAST LORDS OF PALENQUE

It's time to leave the nest. Too soon, it seems to many of us, we leave the planet where we have made our home. We are cast out—by fate or age or maybe by choice—cast out of the nest called Earth. We leave what we know, or we leave what we think we know, for what we think we do not know.

One of the greatest regrets voiced about physical deaths that occur before what is called a "ripe old age" or "the end of a long and full life" is that death has come too soon. Thus the phrase "untimely death" has been coined. Yet the notion that a transition of any sort is untimely dissolves when we remember that all dyings, large and small, major and minor, are part of larger processes.

Die Timely

To encourage the sense that a death is timely, it is important to think of dying at what feels to be the right time. Sometimes this means preparing in advance in order to orchestrate your consciousness throughout the process. Sometimes this means choosing the specific time of transition to a new place or condition. This choice can be made by the consciousness and implemented by thought patterns alone.

This may sound rather odd, even morose, to those who prefer to leave the timing of death to whomever they call God or to fate, rather than saddle themselves with such responsibility. Still, there is value, dignity, self-respect and free will in being able to spot for yourself the right time for you to die. Note that this is not asking you to deny your religious beliefs about God's will regarding your death. Note also that this is not saying that once a time to die is spotted, physical suicide is in order. Note again that there are many forms of death, physical and nonphysical. Creating the dying of a phase of life, an ending for yourself, need not be killing yourself. You always have a choice regarding the way you view both your living and your physical deaths. Let's briefly examine some of the elements of this choice.

Chronological Age Is Deceptive

As suggested in the previous chapter, one of the most important parts of death preparation is knowing where you are in your life cycle. Most people, including school children, who learn about the stages of the life cycle in biology and science classes, assume that being chronologically old is a time when we near the end of our life cycle and that at that time we are nearing death. However, chronological age is deceptive. It indicates very little about critical patterns and cycles in which an individual is immersed. Chronological age leads us to emphasize a biological and linear time aspect of the life cycle, one defined by aging rather than other cyclic aspects of each and every person's life and of each and every person's world.

The life cycle is actually a conglomeration of many other cycles and phases within cycles. For example, the many phases of life and the many living deaths experienced by an individual can be explained in terms of the continuous repetition of: struggles (the ups and downs of life), paradoxes (the trapping conditions in life), insights (the glimpses beyond life's struggles and paradoxes), and various degrees of spiritual elevations (the sustaining of the awarenesses rendered during insights). [These are discussed in Volume One of this series. See Figure 6.1 in this volume.]

The characteristics of a life cycle, a life path, can be examined for indications of these four phases. Each of us can review our lives in terms of the phases we have been through and are in. You can map your life out, noting hundreds of shifts from struggle to struggle to insight to struggle to paradox to spiritual elevation, or whatever path, whatever mixing of these four basic phases, your life takes.

Exercise 6.1: Mapping Your Life

Using, in any order and any quantity, each of the four patterns diagrammed in Figure 6.1 (struggle, paradox, insight and spiritual elevation), map a piece of your life. You can either visualize this map or draw it on paper. You may want to choose a recent week, month, year or decade. You might want to map a relationship or a habit pattern.

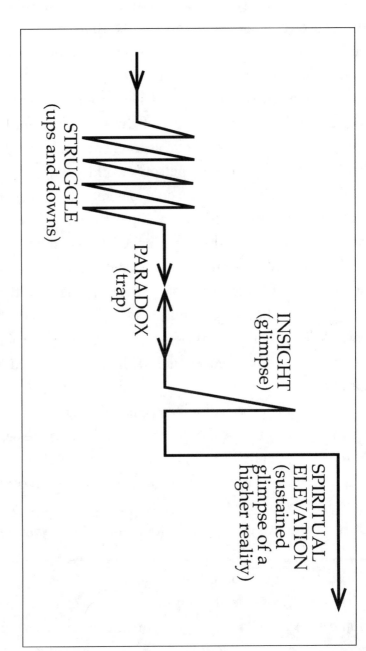

Figure 6.1. Four repeatable and intermixable phases.

You might want to make a general map of your entire life. There is no right or wrong way to do this and no appropriate level of detail. You are the map maker. The territory you are mapping is your own. You will want to do this exercise again many times in your future.

Navigating Paradox with Awareness

Spotting the right time to die or to end a particular phase of life takes a degree of alertness. If we study carefully our patterns and phases, we can detect signs that we have been and are at forks in our life paths, as well as signs that we actually stand before windows of opportunity, avenues that lead to profound transition. Enhancing this awareness can be of great use during the physical death process as well as during all other endings and beginnings. The powerful energy that is released when paradox is navigated with awareness, as diagrammed in Figure 6.2, is valuable and in fact can determine the nature of a transition and the success of a cycling.

A note here: There is indeed energy for change available to us, whether it is merely the energy stored in our immediate cycle or larger energy generated by larger cycles, such as those diagrammed in Figure 6.3. However, accessing energy over which we do not have primary dominion is more complicated and more of a system, population or species process. This energy is that of larger interactions and cycles in which we live.

Let's return to the discussion of our own energy as stored in our own paradoxes. Clearly, when speaking of "our own" energy, it is understood that energy is never actually owned by any single individual. Here, the reference is to what is energy over which an individual has some individual dominion, perhaps

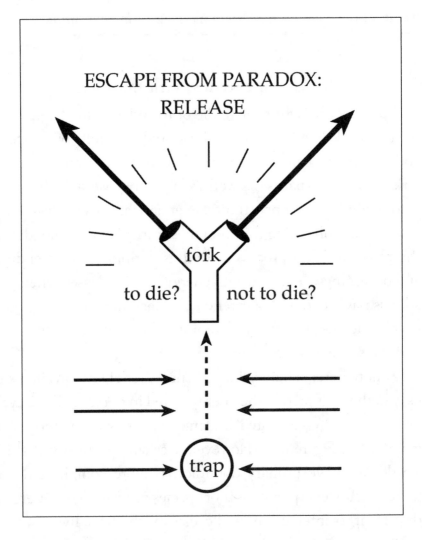

Figure 6.2. Escape from paradox.

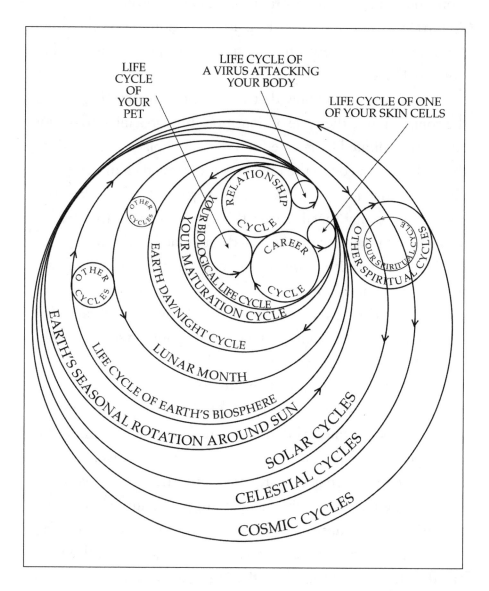

Figure 6.3. Visualization of being part of larger cycles.

more individual dominion than others around that individual. A further discussion of this matter of dominion, retaining dominion and competition for dominion over energy is found in Volume Three.

It is important to know that the post-ending/new beginning, the completion of the cycle or transition through a minor or major death, is facilitated by release from the pause place at the fork in the path. All too often the tendency is to stay stuck in that pause place—in that fork—and not move beyond it. This does not release the energy that is stuck; this does not make that energy available to a new beginning, as is diagrammed in Figure 6.4.

All too often the unreleased energy degrades over time and reaches a point where it is no longer useful or available for release from paradox, as diagrammed in Figure 6.5. Again, this is an indication of the importance of being able to spot the right time to die—the right time to die well.

There are many times when life brings you to a fork in the road. Sometimes you do not see the fork coming—the fork just appears. Sometimes you do not realize that the fork has appeared. You may not be aware of what a fork feels like. You might not realize that you are straddling the forked roads and that you are feeling the imbalancing tug of conflicting choices. Sometimes you realize this but do not want to face this realization. The realization may demand action that you feel unprepared to take. The tug of conflicting choices is, in essence, an *energy paradox*. You are—at least your consciousness matrix is— being pulled in opposing, at least in conflicting, directions.

The pull is actually a push-pull, with the opposing forces equal enough that they counter-pull, reverse and even cancel each other's pull out, something like this steady stuck state:

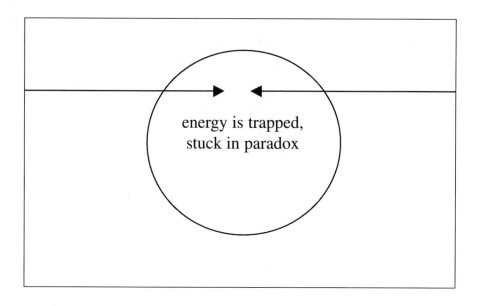

Figure 6.4. Energy remains trapped in paradox.

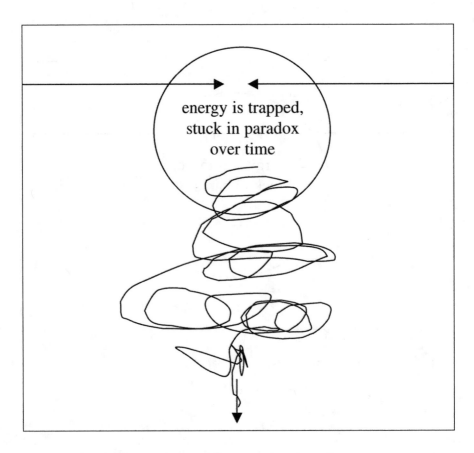

Figure 6.5. Energy stuck in paradox over time degrades.

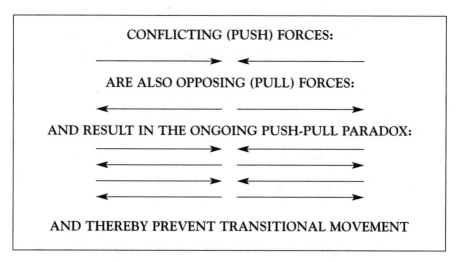

While it is easy to give labels to the conflicting directions found within the pull of opposing or conflicting forces of paradox, paradox is truly a basic energetic state and is best understood as such. We tend to label paradox with particular issues and points of indecision, missing out on the opportunity release from paradox truly presents. For example, any of the following energy traps, each with its own particular labels, falls into a stuck or paradox state:

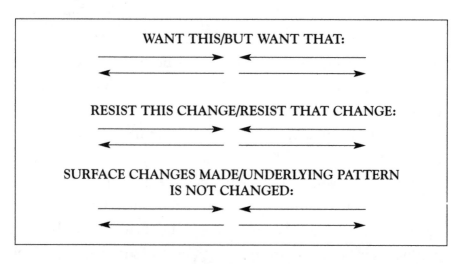

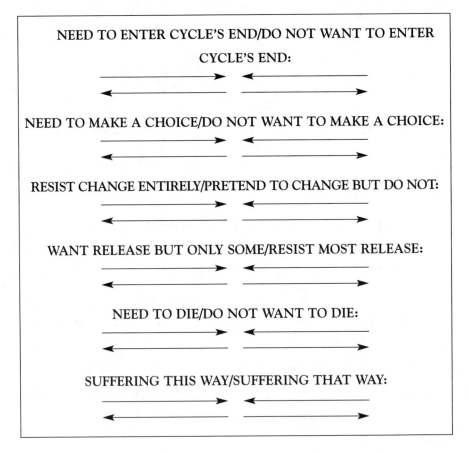

We all know what this feels like—indecision. The experience of indecision is an experience of paradox. And of course, indecision during critical transitions is normal. However, prolonged indecision while not understanding what paradox is and does to a transition can be problematic.

You can get stuck in this personal internally orchestrated tug of war, this energy paradox, for quite some time. When you are stuck this way, your energy is trapped. While this trap may be an interesting place to be, to learn about for a while, it is no place to stay for too long. Many individuals know this and instinctively but relatively unconsciously do something to break out or die out of the trap, or at least to break or die out of it for a while. Unfortunately, such an unconscious breakout may not be as healing, or as pure a release, or as complete, as a more conscious breakout.

We see this all too frequently, for example, in the form of impulsive secret extramarital affairs covered by lies rather than an honest heart-driven resolution to the paradox of a dying or transforming marriage. Another example of an unconscious breakout of a paradox is impulsive suicide as opposed to conscious self-release from a life trap.

Whatever the paradox, despite the anguish you may feel at having to make a choice, with a commitment to die consciously out of a situation or phase of life or out of a physical body, you can rejoice because you are actually at the precious juncture we call *escape from paradox*. A constructive choice to go one way or another can indeed be made. No matter how painful it is to let go, this letting go is your liberation. No matter how much you think you may be losing, you gain your freedom from the paradox.

Gain this freedom wisely, consciously. Open your eyes to the feel of the moment. Again, note that Figure 6.2 shows energy trapped in a paradox, in a double bind, moving toward release in the fork and released in the escape. The nature of this paradox and its possibility for release can be not only sensed but navigated quite consciously.

Exercise 6.2: Developing Fork Awareness

Think of a present, past or possible time in your life when you feel, have felt or will feel substantially unsettled for a significant chunk of time. Be in that time. Do not try to define "substantially unsettled"—just accept whatever comes to mind here. Make the unsettled time you have selected feel like now (if it is not already in the present) by imagining that you are actually feeling that unsettled.

Now stand up, and with your eyes closed, immerse yourself in this situation. Pretend that you are wandering through this situation. With your eyes still closed, take a look under your feet. Try to sense, feel your situation through the soles of your feet. Try to see where you are in your life. Try to see the road or life path you are on. Allow yourself to see that you are at a fork in your path.

Stand before this fork and feel any paradox, double bind, confusion and indecision. If no confusion and indecision comes to you, imagine that you feel these feelings. Explore what these feelings might feel like to you. Feel these feelings. Now exaggerate this confusion and indecision. Hold for the next exercise.

Exercise 6.3: Moving On

At this fork in your life path, inform yourself that you must make a choice to go one way or another—to take one of the roads leading out of the fork. How do you move ahead now? Which way do you go? Force yourself into a decision. Remember that this is just an exercise and you do not necessarily have to take this decision back to your life, your reality outside this exercise.

Make a choice. Choose a road. Close your eyes and let yourself, your consciousness, LEAP into this choice.

Examine your reactions, your feelings here. Do you fully make the LEAP? Or do you hold on to the indecision? The confusion? If so, for how long? What, if any, feelings replace the unsettled sensations you were having? Fear? Shock? Relief? Pride? Exuberance? Anticipation? No feeling? Numbness?

Approaching the Death Juncture

Physical death is a very special juncture, a fork in the path of the self. To die or not to die—this is the question. This same sort of juncture is approached in many areas of life. For example, one's professional life can approach such a juncture. Many who risk their lives in war or in other forms of social duty (such as firefighting) come to forks in their paths. They decide that this risk of their lives is worthwhile in exchange for the service rendered, a service that involves taking this risk. If one is engaged in a continuously risky profession, the decision to risk or not to risk one's life is made frequently. Eventually, it becomes a given. The decision to take the risk is made quickly and almost unconsciously, based upon professional commitment.

Suicide missions, such as those of the Japanese kamikaze pilots, or of freedom fighters on suicide missions, or of those persons who knowingly expose themselves to fatal doses of radiation or bacteria in order to accomplish a task, are slightly different. These choices entail knowing that, upon accepting the duty, one's death is not only possible but almost a certainty. Only a deviation in the process will prevent physical death.

Not all suicide is of such political, social or professional consequence. Not all suicide is conscious. Even the decision to give birth to, to conceive or to live in a physical body in the first place is, in a sense, the initiation of a suicide mission. That physical body will someday die.

Physical life ends eventually. So we might say that choosing to live in a physical body is choosing to do something that most likely or most assuredly includes physical death. Physical death— whether or not a death by conscious present-time choice— moves you past a fork in the road. How? It releases you from the *cycle-subcycle* fork or paradox. Basically, physical death releases you from having to make a choice to repeat the same cycle or subcycle during the same lifetime. (It in no way assures you that you will avoid such repetitions in a later existence.)

See the Way to Cycle Out

To better understand this cycle-subcycle paradox, see yourself at a fork. You can either cycle back into the subcycle you have been in, or cycle out of it into another perhaps grander cycle. Which way do you go? Do you cycle back into this same or a very similar pattern, this same piece of emotional or physical life, or do you cycle out and move on? How do you spot the right time to die, to leave this cycle?

Take a good look at your life cycles and phases. Do not use age as the deciding factor. As noted earlier, too often we surrender to what we have been taught is the biological life cycle and therefore surrender to the notion that disease and aging should determine physical death. We are taught that disease happens, that we are more vulnerable to disease as we age, that the aging process is essential, required, inescapable, is the determinant of the end, and that at the end of the aging process, it is time to die of either disease or old age. But life cycles are not necessarily from birth to old age or disease, and to death.

Life cycles have many beginnings and middles and end points, each of which cycle back into new beginnings. That is why these are called cycles. Quite often a chronological lifetime, moving from traditionally defined birth to traditionally defined death points, includes many life cycles, many cycles through patterns, relationships, behaviors, events, learnings, educations, growths and stages. These are all filled with struggles, paradoxes, insights and spiritual elevations—all full of *choice points*, forks and forks within forks and forks within forks within forks.

At first glance, this cycle-subcycle discussion may cause you to feel a swimming sensation. Where are you anyway? What page of what book are you really on? Which subcycle of which cycle is this anyway? Handle this vagueness by seeing that you can identify your cycles and subcycles, and identify your place in any cycle . . . you can identify the time of beginning, middle and re-cycle, or end of each of your cycles.

You can indeed spot the re-cycle point and the potential for movement beyond a repeating cycle. You can indeed sense a new beginning just past the horizon—just open your eyes. *Spotting the right time to change, transition, die* involves understanding your cycles, being able to gain perspective on your life cycles and their subcycles, in order to gain a long view of all of the cycles in which you have participated—cycles that you feel have been largely yours and cycles of which you have been a small part.

Remember, even your biological life cycle is a subcycle. You are involved in life cycles of the cosmos, of the galaxy, of the solar system, of the planet, of its biosphere, of your species, of your community, of your family, of your children, of your parents, of your siblings, of your closest kin, of your self, of your cells. You are involved in the life cycle of your civilization. You are indeed deeply enmeshed in the life cycle of your reality. [Again, see Figure 6.3 for a visual depiction of cycles within cycles.]

Exercise 6.4: Having Cycle Sensitivity

Single out different personal cycles that you have undergone more than once. List these. These might include repeat performances of falling in and out of love, beginning and ending an academic year, participating in a meeting from start to finish, or entering a race and completing it, as well as many other cycles.

Now single out three life cycles in which you are but a small part and list these. For each of these larger life cycles you have listed, list three smaller cycles or subcycles that take place within those larger life cycles.

There are no right or wrong answers here. Do not worry if you are not sure of what you are doing. Just follow your instincts, follow your own ideas. See your universe as full of cycles and subcycles.

Exercise 6.5: Locating Your Cycles

Now draw or list—place—each personal cycle you identified at the beginning of Exercise 6.4 within the larger cycles you also identified in Exercise 6.4. Do you see where you fit in? Examine the example in Figure 6.3. Draw a similar cycle map for yourself.

Spot the Time

Every cycle has an *omega*, a re-cycle or end point. And every end point is an entry into an *alpha*, a start of a new cycle. Think about the specific although frequently subtle sensations experienced at the ends of your subcycles and cycles. When at an end point, you may feel or see a fork in your path, or you may not detect this fork. You might see an upcoming fork as a death, but only the death of the immediate cycle you are in, because that is what looms largest before your eyes. This looming, while understandably constructed, is an illusion.

You can learn to *see past end points* if you become sensitive to their approach. Here are some means of heightening your sensitivity to the approach of re-cycle or *right time to die* points:

- Become more sensitive to the subtle inputs you give yourself as you get ready to let a part of your life die. Pay attention to very quiet hints, murmurs in your mind that you would normally have missed or totally ignored. Constantly inform yourself of your place on your life path. Close your eyes. Go inside.
- Come face to face with you. Listen, and you will hear what you are telling yourself. Ask quietly, "What am I telling myself?" Don't force it. Just calmly and repeatedly practice this listening, and your inner voice will become more distinct.
- Map your life. Look for simple cycles and for phases and forks. Can you map any of your living deaths? How about the roads leading up to those deaths?
- Always check to see where you stand in your life path. Do you feel unsettled? Is a *cycle exit* or *cycle fork* approaching or already underfoot? Notice where you are and how you feel. Find yourself in the process of living and dying.

Become hypersensitive to your state of mind:

- When you need to shift, your mind moves ahead of you, living at the fork in the road subconsciously before doing so consciously. So notice even slight shifts in your ability to concentrate on your present situation. You (or parts of you) may already have left it.

- As you approach a fork, your energy fluctuates more and more profoundly. So notice even slight changes in your enthusiasm.
- You know when you are trapped in a life paradox, even if you do not want to admit it to yourself. So notice when you feel even *slightly* claustrophobic or trapped—physically, emotionally, intellectually, spiritually.
- Sometimes you make a hidden trap visible to yourself through visible behaviors. So notice if you are regularly exhibiting troubled behavior that is detrimental to yourself or to others.
- Many beings deal with their desire to avoid dealing with the need to let a cycle die by turning off. So notice to what degree you function on automatic—that is, mindlessly.
- Perceived meaning in life may dwindle at re-cycle points. The clarity of meaning becomes muddled at choice points. So notice how you respond when you stop for a moment's reflection and ask yourself, "Who am I and why am I here?"

Why are you here? Is this phase of your life still a rich experience? Or have you stayed in it too long? Is it time to stay or time to go? Give yourself some answers and see if you like them.

Chapter 7

LEAP Level One: Embracing Death

There are cases where faith creates its own verification.
—William James,
THE SENTIMENT OF RATIONALITY

The first and greatest step in a death is the initial recognition and acceptance of its coming—the embrace. This embrace is the first of eight LEAPs in awareness involved in mastering death as presented in this *Continuity of Life* series. This LEAP we speak of here is the fundamental *light-energy-action process* that propels your awareness, your energy, your essence to LEAP into a new reality. We will return again and again to the nature of the LEAP. Here we begin with the first level of the death LEAP: embracing.

Compassion for Your Dying

We hear so much talk about caring, having heart, being loving, being compassionate. However, we very rarely speak about being compassionate with ourselves, about the care and feeding of our own souls. And yet this self-love, unfettered by the claims of the ego but fueled by the respect for the self, is a most essential compassion.

As you enter the prelude to your death, you find yourself undergoing various mental and emotional shifts into new states:

- undergoing *numbing* to avoid the intensity of the experience
- undergoing *overwhelming intensification* of experience and emotion

Extreme One:
Undergoing a Numbing to Experience

Numbness, or some degree of it, is not unusual during endings and deaths. We are all continuously numbing in large and small ways. Quite often, we do not realize that we are doing so, and quite often, the people around us miss this as well. However, even where there is numbness, there may be no outward indication to others or yourself that you are undergoing this numbing of experience. You may unknowingly bury the numbing of experience away from your consciousness. Still, if this is taking place, you are at least undergoing it on some internal level.

In some cases, as one's realization that a death of some part of oneself is coming sets in, detachment begins to grow in one's demeanor, expression and behavior. This detachment is not always pure detachment; instead, it is a combination of detachment, exhaustion, depression, dull anxiety and bewilderment. This combination can look like detachment but be something other than detachment.

Extreme Two:
Undergoing an Intensification of Experience

Intensification—or some degree of it—is also not unusual during endings and deaths. For some, the experience of any transition or death is more than the consciousness can integrate into its usual day-to-day response processing. A deeper response to the experience is taking place, whereas the consciousness integrates only surface elements. While the subconscious is registering how very deep-reaching this experience actually is, the surface behavior of the person undergoing this experience—whether or not conscious of the entire response—is intensifying.

Give Your Transition an Envelope

If you find yourself approaching a death, accept the possibility that your experience may actually fluctuate among the extremes of numbness and intensity for a while. Do not recoil at the sound of this mixed and seemingly chaotic experience. This is your passage into true and healthy detachment (as you will read more about in chapters 16, 17, 18 and 19). This seemingly chaotic experience is also the envelope you create for yourself—an *envelope of containment*, a place where emotional boundaries, no matter how extreme, are set. You can direct your full attention to the emotional body-self you contain within this envelope. You can then direct your compassion there.

Your envelope is permission to be. You can *be* in your envelope. There you can allow yourself to be fully conscious of the death you are undergoing. You can give yourself permission to fully experience and release your feelings about your coming death. *The feelings can flow through you instead of festering within you.* Oftentimes, the permissions you give yourself in your prelude to death are permissions you wished for in life. With permission, you begin to respond with more immediacy than ever, with less holding back, to all that you have been dealing with in your life. You may now take more chances of expression, feel more clearly any fears, feel more fully love, in a richer but increasingly unconditional way.

In the prelude to your physical death, you need for your self the compassion for others that you learned or attempted to develop prior to your dying. *You need all the compassion you can muster for your self as you enter your death transition.* This is in fact true for all your physical and nonphysical dyings.

Spirit Handling

You must strive for a tender, gentle handling of your spirit as you birth it, deliver it into the next dimension of reality. Handle your spirit as you would handle a new baby: most carefully, most lovingly, just as the nourishing mother cradles the new baby in the womb, then in the birth canal as the baby enters this world, then in the world. Cradle yourself as you enter the next world, the beyond, the next phase of your life or death. Begin cradling yourself even during the prelude to this entry into your next phase.

Exercise 7.1: Cradling the Self

The cradling exercise that follows is something that should be practiced frequently. Its gestures are in themselves a great teaching.

If you have been the parent of a young baby or have held a young baby, you may recognize the cradling instinct. You may have felt, quite instinctively, the desire to cradle a baby in your arms and to rock him or her. You might have felt that biological and typically maternal care-and-feeding drive, that love-protection-nurturing drive considered so essential to the survival of offspring. So you may know something about this because you have done some cradling. Or perhaps you have a memory of yourself being cradled as a baby or child.

Whether or not you know much about cradling, imagine now that you are cradling a baby—and that this baby is you. Close your eyes. Hold your arms close to you, as if you have a baby in them, pressing that baby to your chest. Now slowly move those arms further in toward your chest, as if you are embracing yourself. In fact, let your cradling arms hug yourself. That's right, hug yourself, embrace yourself. Let yourself cradle your self, rock your self. Feel as much affection for your self as you can find.

You may find yourself not fully opening to, or holding back some of, or even resisting and balking at this gesture of self-love. Even if you do not think you are resisting, you may be a little stiff or a little lost with the concept of fully embracing yourself. This is all right. It is not unusual to feel rather detached or even uncomfortable embracing your self.

Now, still embracing, just pretend that it is not your self you are embracing; pretend that this is someone other than yourself whom you know and love. Or imagine that you care very much for an imaginary person or an imaginary baby, someone to love right now. Cradle whoever it is, real or imagined. Embrace who it is you choose to cradle. Pour as much nurturing and love as possible into that person, all the while holding yourself. Stay with this process awhile. Hold for the next exercise.

Exercise 7.2: Embracing a Death

Stay in this cradling process of the previous exercise. Imagine that you are taking this soul, this spirit that you are cradling, sheltering it through chaos, danger and fear, through dark hallways, dark pas-

sages, through chambers full of monsters. Imagine that you are strongly protecting that being whom you love with your strong love as you move that being through a series of threatening or unknown environments. Keep cradling. See that you are moving that being through a challenging passage. Inform yourself that this is the death transition of that being.

While you are embracing this being whom you are pouring love into, you are embracing the death of this being, you are embracing the death of this self that you are pouring love into. Hold on very tight. Make your embraces as tight as you comfortably can. Hold for the next exercise.

Exercise 7.3: Embracing Your Death

Wash love over that being. Pour out your love and fully embrace that death. Now, while continuing to lovingly nourish and embrace this dying being, imagine that this being is truly you. Keep loving and hold on. Hold on. Love yourself. Embrace yourself as you go through this transition. Now freeze.

You have just made a LEAP in consciousness. This slight shift (increase or change) in the way you administer compassion to yourself is a significant change—whether or not you register it as one—in your perspective on and thus in your experience of death.

The shift into embracing death—whether it lasts a few moments or stays with you—is a marked shift away from denial of, fear of, anger or other emotions regarding an approaching death. The embracing of death is also more than mere acceptance of and preparation for all your dyings. This is more than a shift in understanding or feeling; it is a *reformatting of the spiritual, mental and emotional structure you have built to relate to life experiences, including death.* This is a structure you have long held in place. Now you are helping emerge within your consciousness this structure of awareness.

Learn to LEAP

Now you have made a LEAP in awareness out of this old structure. A perhaps subtle but yet very new degree and application of light and energy and action have entered your consciousness matrix, shifting that matrix—even if only seeming to shift it very slightly. Your old structure has been shed. It has been reformatted. It has died. While this death may be as subtle and invisible to you as the death of a single-celled animal floating in a large ocean or the death of a few skin cells on your body, this death is actually as profound as you allow it to be.

All death LEAPs, large and small, are great shifts in awareness. When these great shifts last a short while, they are insights, as diagrammed in Figure 6.1. When these shifts stay with you, they are long-lasting insights or spiritual elevations, also diagrammed in Figure 6.1. Ideally, each death LEAP, whether addressing a minor or major transition (death) process, is a lasting spiritual insight, truly elevating the consciousness and sustaining this elevation.

The realization that a LEAP in one's awareness has taken place is key to mastery of death. The LEAP is both a *death technology* and a death in itself. You will note that eight LEAPs are presented in this four volume series. A LEAP serves as a springboard into a new dimension of self, of reality. In this sense, these are LEAPs into shifts in reality, shifts to new dimensions of awareness, what we can call *interdimensional shifts.*

Again, the LEAP is a movement from one dimension of

reality to another. A LEAP is most effective when consciously constructed and purposefully fueled. Then the LEAP lasts, becoming more than a brief insight, becoming a spiritual elevation, a solid steppingstone in your ascension into yet higher consciousness.

A LEAP is a death, in that every shift in awareness, in energy or in degree of light is a death. The more practiced and conscious the dying being is, the cleaner and more powerful and more lasting the death LEAP.

The eight-part death-LEAP series is composed of eight steps that are increasingly profound. Each LEAP is a LEAP you can make in awareness, whether or not you are undergoing a physical death. A LEAP in awareness constitutes a LEAP into a new reality. Each shift in awareness is a shift in the dimension of consciousness in which you find yourself.

Surviving life's most simple and most challenging transitions involves transforming to survive, transcending the given reality or condition. Each LEAP is a release from a particular level of paradox, from a particular level of not knowing the way out of a reality. A LEAP is a break away from ignorance. Figure 7.1 charts and describes the progressive LEAPs detailed in this *Continuity of Life* series.

Embracing Yourself

As simple as it sounds, your full embrace of yourself as you face great change, as you face the death or end of any cycle, is the basic LEAP in awareness necessary to conduct an ending, healthy transition or death. Empathy for yourself and acceptance of the changes you face greatly ease your great passage.

The EIGHT BASIC LIGHT-ENERGY-ACTION PROCESSES (LEAPs)		
LEAP Level	LEAP Type	LEAP Description
One	Embracing	Accepting the cyclic nature of things, accepting with compassion—feeling ready for, fully moving ahead into the death of a phase of life or of the physical body.
Two	Quickening	Raising the vibration or frequency of one's consciousness; pulling together the awareness and energy to effectively travel through transition, even a major transition, or a physical death.
Three	Willing the Exit	Focusing the will in such a concentrated way that the exit from the phase of life or physical body that is perceived as ending or dying is facilitated and consciously navigated.
Four	Leaping to the Next Dimension	Moving the consciousness in such a manner that it LEAPs out of its present dimension of reality, securing a generally developmental exit from that dimension of reality, that phase of life or that physical body the consciousness has been riding in.
Five	Ascending	Moving the consciousness in such a manner that it raises its power—steps, travels, ascends into higher frequencies, higher realms of light, higher dimensions of reality.
Six	Catharting Beyond	Consciously using the energy released by breaking out of a phase of life or physical body to move well beyond the realm of existence being left into a new realm or level.
Seven	Metascending to a New Niche	Realizing the effects of death and ascension without appearing to oneself to have a phase of life or a physical body entirely die, with absolute death receding from the realm of possibility.
Eight	Achieving Metastasis and High Metaxis	Achieving the highest possible range of instantaneous or close-to-instantaneous dimension-shifting or dying out of a phase of life or physical body.

Figure 7.1. The eight LEAPs discussed in the *Continuity of Life* series.

PART II

HOW TO KNOW THE LIGHT

Part II of this book introduces the notion that light is a conceptual tool and that light is so much more than material-reality light. Light is at once a concept, a model, a guiding force and an essence. Light can be understood, clarified, raised to a higher power, reached, via processes that allow us to visualize ourselves clarifying and reaching this higher light. The use of the word "divine" takes on new meaning as we understand tools for sensing or achieving a sense of contact with the divine. The active, consciously perceived, purposefully perceived refining and enhancing of the essence of light fuels transition through, transformation and transcendence of challenges, changes and deaths.

Chapter 8

Becoming Lighter

Now fix your thought upon the Light, and learn to know it.
—*Poimandres to Hermes Trismegistus,*
HERMETICA

Light. Artificial light. Electric light. Translucent light. Night-light. Flashlight. Headlight. Signal light. Spotlight. Strobe light. Light. Light. Light.

Light. Natural light. Dawn's early light. Daylight. Sunlight. Twilight. Moonlight. Starlight. Northern light. Firelight. Light. Light. Light.

Light. Love-light. Divine light. Etheric light. White light. Galactic light. Cosmic light. Light. Light. Light.

Know That Light Is More

We take what we think of as light for granted. It pours in through windows, filters in through canopies of leaves in forests, reflects off moons and lakes and mirrors, comes on with the flick of a switch. Yet light is much more than the human eye can see. In fact, what the human eye sees of light is a hint of what is really there. Human seeing of light serves as training material for a greater vision of, a widening of the perception to a much broad-er range of light, which includes forms of light not picked up by our biological eyes. Indeed, this greater vision is not dependent upon the biologically contrived optical organ, the eyeball, and its biologically contrived transmitter, the optic nerve. Instead, this vision is dependent upon enhanced perception.

It is time to see light with new eyes. What we think of as light in material-plane reality is a small fraction of what light is. (Whether your access to this notion is via your imagina-tion or via your belief system, simply work with these ideas in whatever form you choose: metaphor, imagination or a personal or spiritual reality.) Light is a powerful essence, something far greater than physical sensory organs can regis-ter. Light can transform appearances; therefore, in at least this way, light can alter that which it casts upon. Light can both feed and dispel illusions. With care and knowledge of the processes involved, we can see that light can transform matter, including flesh; light can heal that which it touches and fills; light can be an elixir; light can be a salve; light can touch and affect the frequencies of solid objects and of living things.*

The more defined and focused the light, the greater its force. Focusing compresses the complexity of light into power. Light is at once the wave and the particle, the author and the author's document, the formula and the product of the formula.

---

* While modern science has developed light-technology tools such as the laser beam (which can be directed to bend, to cut into, to materially affect the matter it beams into) and the use of light in treating various medical conditions, the use of light in working with matter and in healing has many other faces.

Darkness Has a Character

We tend to think of light as having a multitude of qualities and of darkness as being nothing much more than the absence of light. Try turning this idea around for a moment. What if light were merely the absence of darkness and darkness were the opposite? This is difficult to imagine because we are more aware of *sources of light*: suns, stars, man-made light fixtures. We do not think in terms of sources of darkness and darkness existing in several dimensions (although perhaps it would help us to recognize that such sources exist and that darkness seeps, emanates, spews from these).

This discussion is intended to enhance your awareness of and appreciation for light. The reason this enhanced awareness of light is valuable is that it enables you to think in terms of *becoming more like light.* You must have a feel for the nature of light to allow your imagination (as imagination is a valuable tool) to raise your physicality toward light—and toward a less dense consistency than matter. *Your imagination can lead you in this direction and in the necessary transformation.* Understand that the light you see in the material plane is what the purer light can filter into your atmosphere. Still, there is additional light to see beyond the constriction of the physical plane. Released from physicality, light is freer. Light increases as density decreases. [See Figure 8.1.]

A note here: The concept of physicality is a stumbling block for some people. Let's speak here in terms of what we call physicality to further impress this upon you who feel you are living primarily or entirely in the material (physical) dimension of reality: Being physical, having density to the degree that you are physical, *is not an absolute characteristic of existing but one of*

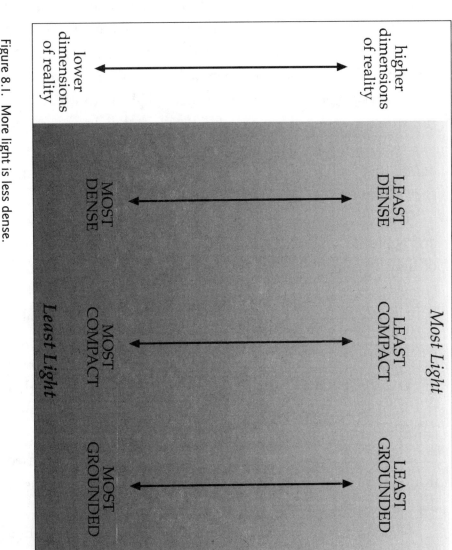

Figure 8.l. More light is less dense.

many possible characteristics. You can exist without physicality and without the relationships you have developed in the physical world. Hold onto this concept at all times. You see,

THE LIFE FORCE DOES NOT DIE.

Know Density

A deep feel for density (as depicted simply in Figure 8.1) eases your passage from physical death into the beyond. Knowing that physical death is a moving through *realms of density* is knowing that death is not the end of your existence but the transformation of your existence from one degree of density to another. Again,

THE LIFE FORCE DOES NOT DIE.

Density is a critical concept. Understanding that there are gradations of density allows you to understand how your addictions to, your dependencies upon, your reality (your programmings and patternings) can be put to death, transcended, even while you still live in your physical body. Physical programmings have densities. They are frequently embedded in the physical body's genetic code at the cellular level, as well as in the neurological system, the spinal fluid and other physical sites. Physical and other energetic programming can be altered or suspended when it is raised—ascended into—a less dense, lighter state.

Try not to overintellectualize the concept of density. Misunderstanding reality is one of the dangers of thinking too narrowly (what may seem to be logically) about important concepts. Just allow these ideas about density and ascending into less dense states to be with you. After a while, these ideas will be comprehensible in a visceral way.

The following exercises will teach you, awaken your consciousness to the *intuitive technology* required to travel to other realms of density.

Exercise 8.1: Becoming Less Dense

Close your eyes. Imagine that your body is turning to liquid: at first a thick syrupy liquid, then a liquid that becomes thinner and thinner. Imagine that this liquid becomes lighter as it thins and that it eventually turns to fluid light. Feel that you are becoming glowing liquid.

Now let this liquid become vaporous, misty, and then more vaporous and more glowing. You are turning to light. As you turn to lighter and lighter light, you become less and less dense. You move into higher realms of light—realms of light into which only light can travel.

See these realms of light as layered from darker to lighter. Move on up through them, toward the lightest light.

Beings, life forms, take on varying degrees of density. A life form locates along a continuum of most dense to least dense. However, you are seeing that you can move your self along this continuum. Fluid light has far less density than any material liquid such as syrup or water. Vaporous light has almost no density whatsoever, and immaterial light no density. Imagine that you feel a tingling as you leave your states of density, as you shed your layers of density.

The practice above trains you to evolve your consciousness, and it trains you to transition or die smoothly. As you grow in the consciousness of light, your awareness, your mentality itself becomes less dense and thus more expanded. This development can feel rather ungrounding to those new to this process, because gravity will have a diminishing pull on your thoughts and thus on your body. This ungrounding is a positive step, albeit initially disorienting. Within (and across) each dimension of reality, the life forms capable of shifting at will across the broadest range of densities are most evolved at transition, at death, at interdimensional travel.

Exercise 8.2: The Light Diet

Repeat the previous exercise, but now take it more slowly and in greater detail. Inch your awareness very slowly up the scale of decreasing density. Imagine you are changing very slowly from purely and densely physical into increasing lightness—degrees of light. Notice the sensation that you are losing weight. You are, but perhaps not in the traditional way.

As this unweighting takes place, the actual diminishing of your body relative to the expansion of your energy begins. Take some time to think about this: the diminishing of your body.

Say this aloud: "The diminishing of my body . . ." and see yourself shrinking. Now say, "Relative to my expanding lightbody." See your lightbody growing larger here. Your physical body is diminishing when compared to your expanding lightbody. Relax.

If you are enjoying this sensation, think about what you are enjoying about it. Some of us enjoy ungrounding feelings, such as roller coaster rides. Some of us do not. This exercise may feel similarly unsettling, perhaps even dizzying, if practiced with great concentration. You may be experiencing some of the initial sensations of gravity-lifting.

This decohesion, or diminishing cohesion, is normal. Your physical bits are sticking together less. This is conscious entropy. Entropy is the tendency of a physical system to spin out, dissolve, disintegrate, wear down and, in this sense, be perceived by some as dying.

You are engaging in conscious entropy, which is a bit different in that the dissolving of physicality is being consciously conducted—by you. This is all right. You can change your makeup substantively this way. Tell yourself, "I change this way."

Linger in these sensations and concepts awhile, allowing your imagination to lead you wherever it takes you.

Your mastery of your minor and major transitions involves focus on matrix changing. Your matrix changing requires your ability to shift densities, first in your imagination and then in your essence. (Recall the discussion of the matrix that your consciousness creates—this is your *consciousness matrix*. This matrix drives all your actions, behaviors, operations and interactions.) You can learn this matrix changing by giving your mind suggestions, by practicing, imagining that you are becoming lighter, less dense, as in the previous exercises. As the physical matter of "you" becomes, in your mind's eye, less tightly organized, *less rigidly structured in a material sense*, it has the opportunity to become more complex in a multidimensional sense. As matter becomes less physical, less dense, it weighs less and less per cubic millimeter in relation to the expanse of the energy it emits—its energy body—and is thus in relative terms less weighed down.

Exercise 8.3: Metaphysical Calisthenics

Imagine that you are shrinking physically and then expanding physically. Practice this shift several times.

Now imagine that you are shrinking physically while expanding in light form. See yourself becoming an increasingly luminous, beautiful form of pure light as you expand.

Feel relief—or imagine that you feel relief—as your physicality diminishes, as if you are shedding a tattered, heavy and unnecessary coat. After a while, your physical body is very tiny and your beautiful lightbody fills a huge space, streaming everywhere within that space. Try to maintain this light-form sensation as long as you can, even after you complete this particular exercise.

**REMEMBER,
A CONSTANT STREAM OF LIGHT
CAN STILL THE DARK.**

Chapter 9

Understanding Love and Light

May the long time sun shine on you
All light surround you
And the pure light within you
Guide your way on.
—Incredible String Band, "Longtime Sunshine"

Darkness lets you appreciate its absence. Darkness lets you appreciate light. But what exactly is darkness the opposite of, if anything?

Suffering lets you appreciate its absence. Suffering lets you appreciate love. But what exactly is suffering the opposite of, if anything?

Why are the absence of suffering and the presence of love so closely linked? Could suffering and love be experiential opposites? Or are they experiential antidotes?

Turn Suffering Around

Think in terms of a very pure, a wholly pure love, an entirely

unattached and unconditional love. Unconditional love, un-
like emotional love, is virtually free of all physical-plane-based
attachment. On the other hand, emotional love—which is
(even while denying this) at least somewhat if not entirely
attached and conditional—opens the door to suffering en-
trenched in and fueled by attachment to the physical body, to
the emotions, the material world, one's own particular physical-
plane reality. This is not to decry emotional love, which can be
an intensely positive experience. This is to invite you to fully
distinguish the difference between attachment-based love and
attachment-free love. Emotional love is most certainly a most
misunderstood sensation. This is because it gets mixed in with
attachments and too frequently with the suffering of troubled
attachments.

The good feeling of pure, unconditional, unfettered love is
yours for the asking. You carry its seeds within you. Nourish
the seeds, and your heart can open like a window. An abundant
goodness, a beautiful energy, a love-light can flow from within,
from without, and through and around you. The sweet mists of
love—a very pure kind of love—can fill your atmosphere.

You can use what you read here to help you generate this
sort of positive ambience or presence within you and around
you, in order to help you take a positive approach to the challenges you face. Herein we focus on the development and mag-
nification of positive feelings about change, transition, transformation and death. Although it is quite natural to experience a
range of feelings about intense changes and deaths, these transitions are navigated best when a positive approach is taken.

By positive approach, we do not imply a superficially positive
approach but instead a deeply felt, thoroughly assimilated positiv-

ity. For those readers currently enduring a certain or even a high degree of mortal suffering (physical or emotional), be reminded that the positivity called for here is not going to be arrived at through rational or intellectual means. A feel (which is more like an intuitive flash than a logical deduction) for what the positivity of love-light is really about can help still your pain. And again, note that *a constant stream of light can indeed still the dark.*

Sensory Mixings

Love and light are simple words. We all think we know what they mean. You "fall" in love and you "turn on" the light—right? Love is something you feel and light is something you see—correct? Well, yes, right and correct, at least in as much as a material-plane resident might tend to believe—at least this much. However, love and light are so much more than your standard physical senses may detect.

No matter how rich your material-plane sensory intake, you are relatively blind and deaf, more like numb to the most valuable data coming to you. This is part of your long-standing confinement to, even imprisonment in, the material plane. It is time now for you to access the intelligence that is rightfully yours. It is time to see, to hear, to truly feel what is here: access to higher forms of love and light.

A different use of your five senses—or of what it is you think you perceive with your five senses via sensory input, via seeing, hearing, smelling, tasting and touching—is required now. Only this change in what you have known to be "sensation" will enable you to get, to grok, to absorb the pure love and light you need, and to see the very fine relationship between love and light. You can work your way into an enhanced awareness of higher forms of love and light by training your senses to take in new forms of information.

How so? As you amp up your perceptual abilities, you will find that you mix sensory modalities. You will hear colors, feel sounds, see feelings. At first this might feel as if it is not really happening—as if it is an optical, auditory and/or emotional illusion. However, as you move into what you think of as the world of illusion, you make room for what you have previously excluded from your reality because the material-plane reality told you it was so illusory, so unreal, so imaginary, so very not credible to you. You are actually moving away from the illusion you have thought of as your reality, a step closer to another reality.

Exercise 9.1: Sensory Mixing

Choose a color you see in your environment. Focus on that color. Now close your eyes. Imagine what this color would sound like if you could hear it. . . . Now imagine what it would taste like. . . . Now imagine that you are moving (walking, swimming, flying) through this color. What would this color feel like to the touch? What would it feel like to move through?

Exercise 9.2: Multisensory Mixing

Pick your favorite color or a color that you know well for this exercise. Close your eyes. Try to see this color in your mind's eye. As you do so, imagine that you are hearing it, tasting it, smelling and feeling it, all at the same time. Do this for many minutes. Work to run the different sensory modes (such as hearing, feeling, tasting, smelling) at the same time.

Eventually feel that you have become the color. You sound, feel, taste and smell like the color. You are now vibrating the color.

Altered Sensory States as Portals

When experimenting with the mixing of sensory modalities—sensory mixing—you might feel slightly confused, disoriented. Stay calm. This passes.

You have produced an altered state of awareness for yourself by running messages such as "blue" or "hot" or "soft" or "loud" through different mental pathways than your brain has set up for them, and by running more than one of these rerouted messages at once. Knowing how to consciously create for yourself an altered state or a new state of awareness is one of your *keys to new kingdoms*. Recognize that the altered states you pass into and through can be openings—or what you might consider windows or passages—into heightened awareness. We can call such openings portals—portals into the next or another level of knowing.

Your increasing ability to recognize the higher realms of the purer love and purer light will be an increasingly valuable guide for you. Even in your darkest hour, the faintest love-light you find within even the deepest recess of your soul will be your guiding beam. Hook into the highest, least-dense frequency, the purest energy you can find, and hang on. The illumination you seek, the true love-light, is already within you, ready to guide your way on. Just follow your light.

Chapter 10

Romancing the Light

A point I saw which
rayed forth light so keen,
needs must the vision that it flameth on
be closed because of its strong poignancy. . . .
—Dante Alighieri,
THE DIVINE COMEDY

Come to know the light intimately before you die. You can do this. The light you seek is so powerful and so omnipresent that it can come in through any and all of your sensory organs and it can come into your awareness without involving any of your physical sensory organs. This light is so potent that you can detect its presence with or without your biological eyes seeing it. You can feel it, hear it, sense it, see it, even with your eyes closed.

Indeed, you can even taste the higher light. You can savor its sweet nectar when it comes to you, a glowing stream wafting into your consciousness. You taste, you feel, you see as much of this higher light as you can access, as you can absorb, as you can believe or even imagine exists.

Opening Windows

The more adept you are at all forms of dying, the greater your contact with the highest, purest form of light. This is because the mastery of death transitions involves opening to the multiple dimensions of reality and of density. With but a little practice, any time you wish it to, your heart can open like a window onto amazingly extensive goodness, allowing the sweet mists of what seems to be otherworldly, other-reality light to descend upon you and into you. You can fall in love with the high light. This light is yours; it is your lover. This is the guiding beam to seek, the river to ride, amidst any storm, any challenging transition, any death.

So learn death as you have a right to know it: *death into light.* Shed your blindness. Shed what you know of as your life. This may at first be difficult. This is because the stream of your reality, your daily life, engulfs you and even fools you. That stream is merely an illusion. That this stream ends in a final death with nothing beyond it is merely an illusion. Learn to see beyond the false walls of what you may define as your reality. After all,

THE LIFE FORCE DOES NOT DIE.

Exercise 10.1: Feeling Your Engulfment

Pause now. Close your eyes. Feel for a moment how very engulfed in what you think of as your reality you are. See what you have been defining as your world. Do not, for this moment, look beyond your so-called world. However, try to see its boundaries, its walls.

You are a participant in a massive escalation in awareness. *You already know* far more than you realize you know. You have already glimpsed the beyond and seen the light. You already know that the beyond is only beyond so long as it is beyond your perception. Your perception is expanding to see so much more now. Whatever you see, there is more . . . to see. Let your eyes open—your higher eyes.

Exercise 10.2: Seeing the Mists

The beyond is here now. It surrounds you. Its sweet mists waft subtly into your material world. Close your eyes, and you will see this. You will see that you are already immersed in the beyond, that the beyond is always here.

With your eyes closed, allow yourself to imagine that the light mists of another world are flowing into yours. These are the light mists of your world.

Should you doubt this imagery of light, should you disbelieve its veracity, temporarily suspend your disbelief. Just imagine that you believe in and see this light for a while. You can return from this imagery of light misting into your "real" world at will. There is thus no risk in exploring this possibility. Believe in and see, experience, the light mists flowing in around you. Hold for the next exercise.

Exercise 10.3: Examining the Light

Your eyes are still closed. Again see the misty light flowing in from another world. Note your doubts, if any, regarding the realness of this light.

With your eyes still closed and while looking at or imagining that you see the light mist, organize your doubts into a quiet system, grouping these doubts and maybe even noting which are main doubts and which are sub-doubts.

Continue seeing the mist, the light mist. Imagine that your doubts about the realness of the light mist are being written onto a chalkboard on wheels. Once you have vaguely organized your doubts, think of them as a body of information that can be held, with great respect, off to the side for a while. See yourself pushing the rolling chalkboard off to the side.

You can see now beyond this list of doubts into a special place. This place is full of information about the nature of light. This place is full of light! Each piece of light is a bit of information, an idea about light.

Allow all these bits of information, whether imaginary or real to you, to come in to your awareness. Savor these ideas. Experience them. Enjoy them as wonderful possibilities, utopian dreams or fragments of fairy tales, if that is how you wish to have yourself see this imagery of light. Just practice seeing the light and knowing it. Hold for the next exercise.

Exercise 10.4: Dancing with Light

Now, with your eyes still closed, imagine that a mist of light flows to a place right in front of you. Reach into this light with your hands. With your eyes still closed, imagine that you stand—or if you wish, actually do go ahead and stand—to greet this light.

Treat this light as a dance partner. Imagine that you are dancing with this light, or actually do begin to physically dance with this light. As you dance, see yourself swirl with your light partner into a paradise full of light—whatever that paradise may be to you.

Dance on for a while. Then freeze. Note how you feel.

Chapter 11

Clarifying the Light

What is happening during the process of dying, with its outer and inner dissolution, is a gradual development and dawning of ever more subtle levels of consciousness . . . the process moves gradually toward the revelation of the very subtlest consciousness of all: the Grand Luminosity or Clear Light.

—Sogyal Rinpoche,
THE TIBETAN BOOK OF LIVING AND DYING

What is divine? It is whatever is most holy, most supremely respected by you. Encourage yourself to define divinity for yourself, and then aspire to know what you feel is most divine. This is an effective way to nourish your spirit, your essence. This is where a feel for the meaning of light is essential. You can use your understanding of high light to help define what you know of divinity. The essence of divine light is something you must see with your inner eye to appreciate.

Invoke the Light

As you begin to actively look for and call upon the stream of high or divine light, you grow increasingly sensitive to its presence. This is a circular process. From this point of increased sensitivity to light, you increase the amount of higher, divine light that you feel is available to you.

YOU CHOOSE TO SEE MORE LIGHT ⟶

YOU SEE MORE LIGHT.

YOU SEE MORE LIGHT ⟶

YOU CHOOSE TO SEE YET MORE LIGHT.

You do raise the light you access by increasing the frequency of your energy, the sort of energy with which you call upon the light. This *invoking the light* is a special sort of prayer. This prayer does not pray that someone takes care of you, that someone sends you light and hope. Instead, this form of prayer places the responsibility on you to find the light and thus also gives you direct access to the light.

The actual seeking and the accessing of the higher light is all that is required to put you in touch with what we are calling the divine. The reason this is so simple is that the essence of divine light is available to you whenever you call upon it. Actually, this light is always present; you need only recognize it and let it in. *Open the window. Call upon the light. Invoke the light and you see it. Step into the light.*

Opening the window onto the divine light is like opening the curtains and even the window of a darkened room, and allowing the sunlight to pour in. But this window to the divine light is not in the wall of a building. *This window is in the wall of your reality.* And this window *is* your reality, so you can install this window and open it whenever you are ready.

Exercise 11.1: Reading the Atmosphere

With your eyes open, examine the space (or atmosphere) in front of you. Reach out and run your fingers through it.

Leave your hands out in front of you and close your eyes. Imagine that your fingertips have become supersensitive.

Run those fingertips through the air and imagine that you feel variations all around you, the differences in the density, the seeming thickness, of the air. You may find pockets of emptiness, less-dense spaces where your hands reach or move differently. Move your hands delicately to maximize their sensitivity.

Also imagine that you feel subtle streams of air or energy moving past your fingertips. Allow your fingertips to follow these imaginary streams. Continue feeling the atmosphere with your fingers into the next exercise, opening your eyes as you do.

Exercise 11.2: Breaking Through

Now imagine that the atmosphere in front of you is opening— cracking a little or tearing gently. Reach into the opening with your fingertips and pull the opening further open. As you do this, imagine that what pours in through the crack is a very different, far brighter, far lighter gleaming atmosphere.

The splendid gleam continues to pour in and fill the space you are in. You are soon immersed in this new atmosphere, and you love it. Something about the light that is pouring in is so clean, so pure, so refreshing, so far beyond the light you have been seeing with your eyes in your daily life—your material-plane reality.

You feel the light filling your eyes until everything you see looks to be of this light. If this is difficult to visualize with your eyes open, close your eyes now to see more.

This accessing of the higher light, as simple as it sounds (and as imaginary as it may seem to some of you), is important training for you. You are basically training your sensitivity. You can use this sensitivity, call upon it in many different situations, both in- and out-of-body, during minor and major endings and transitions—including during and likely even after physical death. You can use your sensitivity to the high light to find your way through any difficult life transition, to navigate your way out of any trap and paradox. When you feel emotionally trapped or blocked, you can remain in the situation as long as you need to, and then you can open the atmosphere you are in and allow another atmosphere to pour in and engulf you. You can even do this or imagine that you are doing this during physical death.

Clarify the Light

Remember that the light you see is as pure and as divine as you are able to let yourself see it being. This is why learning to clarify the light you see is important. You must learn to *raise the purity of the light you see to the highest, cleanest, most divine level possible.* You must also notice when the light you see does not rise to the highest levels of purity.

Exercise 11.3: Enhancing the Light

Close your eyes. Scan the back of your eyelids. Notice that what you see with your eyes closed is not an even field. There are degrees of, shades of and sometimes even colors of dark and light there. Sometimes the degrees are so very subtle that they are hard to detect, but they are always there.

With your eyes still closed, roll your eyeballs up as far as they will go, as if you are looking at the inside of your forehead. While in this

---

position, close your eyes even tighter. Keep the eyes closed tightly, and hold the eyeballs rolled back. Now, with your eyeballs still rolled back and your eyelids still closed, relax the tightness of the lids. Now tighten the closed eyelids again. Continue this way, loosening and tightening your closed eyelids, always with your eyeballs rolled back. Loosen. Tighten. Look for variations in the light you see on the insides of your eyelids or in your interior visual field. Hold for the next exercise.

Exercise 11.4: Clarifying the Light

Keep your eyes closed. Choose the lightest area or bit of light you have been able to find during the scanning you have been doing in the previous exercise. Find this light again. It may appear to float around. Do whatever you can to follow it or re-invoke it with your eyeballs. If you cannot follow it or re-invoke it, that is all right—just find another bit of light or create a bit of light to focus on by imagination or by memory.

Gaze at this piece of light. Imagine that it becomes brighter and expands. Enjoy whatever colors you see in this light, if any. Stay with this light, focus on it, even if it changes. Continue raising its brightness and lightness, however that appears to you.

Now exercise your mind's eye. Transform the light you are studying to something even more expanded and lighter and brighter than it has been. If your light is color light, try turning it to white light. If your light is white or when it becomes white, try whitening and brightening it further. Examine it for purity. Is it an evenly bright light? Can you brighten up its darker areas or streaks? Stay with the light. Re-invoke it if needed.

With your eyes still closed, clarify this light. Clean it with your energy as you run your examining inner eye through it, as if your examining inner eye were a rake or a grid. Clean the light. Clarify the light. Remove any dense, dark or irregular areas of uneven light. Again, use your imagination wherever needed.

As you clarify the light, find yourself feeling more and more pleased with it, and more and more attracted to it. Create a light as pure as you deem possible.

Chapter 12

Praying as Practical Action

Behold, I will do a new thing: . . . I will even make a way in the
wilderness, and rivers in the desert.

—Isaiah 43:19

The usefulness of prayer is vastly underestimated, because prayer is vastly misunderstood. Basically, praying is a way of focusing one's energy on realizing possibilities. Prayer tends to want to reach outside of what appears to be the reality, or perhaps the material plane, for a desired outcome. Prayer takes many forms, ranging from: asking a god or a higher power for assistance; extending one's own or another force's protection, blessings and good wishes to oneself or others; reaching into other dimensions for guidance; and invoking light or energy to generate a shift in a given reality.

Prayer to Invoke

All methods of prayer seek to engender a particular state of mind in the praying individual, a state of mind that allows for a shift in awareness.* All too often, the power in the basic act, even in the literal physical gesture of praying, is overlooked. The following exercises are an explanation of prayer as practical action as well as prayer as a method of deliverance into other dimensions or aspects of reality. These basic exercises can be repeated—in actuality or by one's consciousness—again and again in life and through all minor and major emotional and physical endings, transitions and dyings.

Exercise 12.1: Inscribing Prayer Gesture in Your Energy Memory

Place your hands together, fingertip to fingertip, palm to palm, flat against each other. Hold your hands as they are placed together directly in front of your chest, with your elbows bent. Feel your hands touching each other. Get a sense of what this feeling is. Try to become very aware of it. Close your eyes and feel your fingertips and hands pressing together. [See Figure 12.1.]

You will never forget this feeling. This feeling, whether or not you have hands to place together, whether or not you have a physical body at a time you might want this feeling, can always be replicated in your energy memory. With your eyes still closed, hold this position for many minutes.

Exercise 12.2: Practicing Ascension Prayer Motion

Now, with your hands still pressed together, push them more intensely into each other. Slowly, very slowly, raise that prayer— raise those hands in prayer position—up along your central vertical axis, which is in front of your body but parallel to your backbone.

---

* Some forms of prayer seek to involve such a state of mind in others. This can occur when one person prays for another wanting to help or attract an improved or positive outcome to that other.

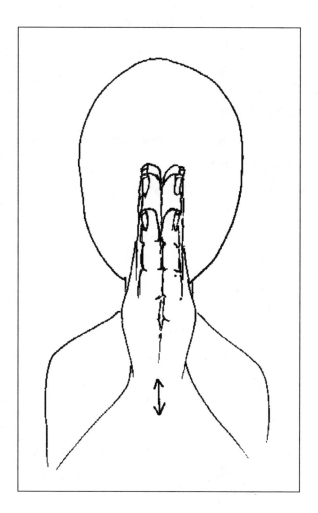

Figure 12.1. Prayer gesture.

Keep those hands in this prayer position all through the exercise.

Move your praying hands from a lower point in front of your chest further upward, remaining parallel to your spine. Move your prayer along your vertical axis as it goes up in front of your throat, up in front of the center of your face. Keep raising your hands, still in prayer position, fingers still pointing toward the area above your head, until they are located above your head, as in Figure 12.2. Hold a moment.

Now, very slowly, move your hands back down, holding the prayer position. Keep those hands vertical along your vertical access, moving them downward in this vertical position as far as they will go.

Do this entire motion—up and down—ten times. Complete the exercise with the hands still in prayer position in front of your chest. Hold for the next exercise.

Exercise 12.3: Practicing Open Ascension Prayer Motion

With the hands in the prayer position in front of your chest, focus for a moment on the ridge of your knuckles in each hand. Move these two knuckle ridges away from each other, pulling the palms of the praying hands away from each other but leaving the fingertips and wrists in contact. Your hands are still in the prayer position, but you have created an open space, a special space, a sacred vessel between the palms. Try to form a diamond-shaped space between your two still-touching hands (as in Figure 12.3).

Now go through the exercise described above (Exercise 12.2), moving those hands vertically in prayer position—but now in this opened up prayer position. Hold when you reach the highest point above your head.

Move your open prayer up and down your vertical access several times. Complete the exercise with your hands still in open prayer

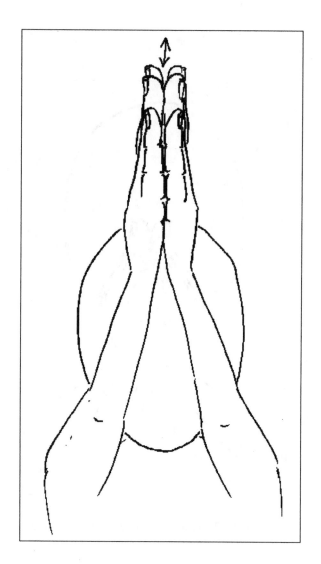

Figure 12.2. Extended prayer gesture.

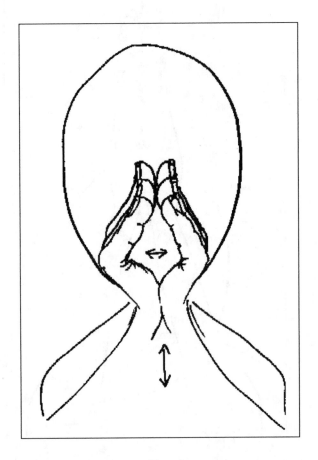

Figure 12.3. Open ascension prayer gesture.

position, with the diamond-shaped space still between your palms, with your praying hands back in front of your chest. Hold this position for the next exercise.

Exercise 12.4: Creating a Sacred Vessel for Yourself

Begin in the position in which you completed the previous exercise. Your open-praying hands forming the diamond-shaped space are in front of your chest. Focus on that enclosed space between your hands.

Imagine that you are in that diamond-shaped space between your palms. Imagine climbing in if you have to. It may be hard for you to imagine that your entire body is in that space. If it helps, imagine that you have shrunk in size and that your entire body is actually able to fit into that space. Otherwise, just take your consciousness—the part of yourself that has no body, your self, the idea of your mind—into that space. Hold this position and thought for the next exercise.

Exercise 12.5: Moving Your Sacred Vessel

Now repeat the motion of the earlier exercise [Exercise 12.3], in which you moved your praying hands (open prayer position) along your vertical access, up in front of your throat, in front of the central part of your face, up parallel to your forehead and out above your head. All the while, hold very, very carefully your self-awareness, your consciousness, in that space between your palms.

Now, very slowly, very deliberately, pull your hands and your self back down to the space in front of your chest. Feel as if you are protective of your self as you do this.

Repeat this exercise several times, attempting each time to pull more and more of your focus, more of your attention, into the space between your palms. Feel as if you have left your body and are now just living between your palms. Eventually return your praying hands, your sacred vessel, to the position in front of your chest. Hold for the next exercise.

Exercise 12.6: Releasing from Your Vessel

Repeat the previous open prayer exercise, in which you are moving your sacred prayer vessel with all your attention, your self, your consciousness, between the palms with which you form this vessel. This time move your hands ever more slowly, as slowly as possible while still moving, up along the vertical access, up and up, up as far as they will go, without undoing your open prayer position, stretching way up above your head. Hold your self between your palms, way up there. Hold there.

Your consciousness is now up there in the diamond-shaped space between your palms. Focus on this consciousness. Attempt to strengthen, to make more potent, more clear, your consciousness as it sits there above your head between your palms. With concentration, expand yourself between your palms, so much so that you begin to push on the inside of your palms, pushing, pushing, as if trying to push your hands apart from each other because your self is too large for that space now.

Now, very gently, very slightly, separate your hands. Let the palms and fingers and wrists be near each other but not touching. Stretch your hands out above your head a little further, with the hands now being stretched parallel to each other, parallel and untouching (as in Figure 12.4). If you are lying down, consider this reaching upward as a moving toward the area beyond the top of your head. If you are sitting or standing, reach for the sky. Hold your reaching with the parallel untouching palms position. Take a deep breath. Hold that breath a moment.

Now, as you release that breath, see yourself escape upward from

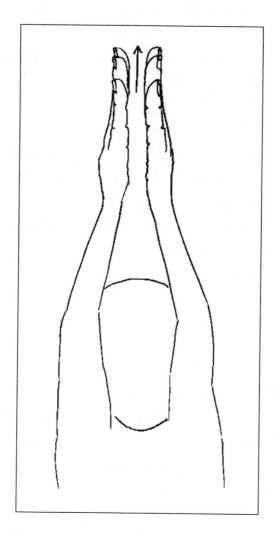

Figure 12.4. Deliverance prayer gesture.

between those hands. Stay with your escaping self. Keep going upward, out beyond the top of your head. Out. Out. Out. Continue this ascending, this climbing. Notice what you imagine happens to that self, that idea of your self, that has escaped from between those palms.

Exercise 12.7: Delivering Your Self

Pull your consciousness back to your hands. Return your self to the space between your parallel hands above your head. Now place your fingertips and wrists back together.

Your conscious is between your palms now. Slowly pull your self back down in front of your chest, still between your palms. Hold your self there, being very aware that you are between your palms.

Now aim the point created by your fingertips in various directions other than beyond the top of your head, other than upward—rather, directly in front of you, downward, to the side at various angles.

Pick, imagine a beautiful, serene spot where you would like to send your self, to send the self still between your palms. This spot can be upward, downward, sideward, very far away or somewhere very near. Move your palms, still closed at your fingertips and wrists, with your self concentrated between them, toward that space as far as you can reach. Hold a moment.

Then, as if you were releasing a baby, separate your fingers and wrists, separate your hands slightly so that they are parallel. Take a deep breath. Hold a moment. Now slowly relax and breathe out. As you do so, deliver yourself into that space you have chosen for your self. Imagine that you have entered a beautiful, serene and very safe space. Know that you have taken very good care to deliver your self, your consciousness, your attention, into this safe space.

Breathe a sigh of relief. Stay in this place. Hold for the next exercise.

Exercise 12.8: Returning to Center

Stay there in your safe space. Develop a detailed picture of that place. Use your imagination to enhance this picture. Pull as much light as you can into this picture.

Explore the space. What does it look like? What can you do there? Where is it? How does it feel to be there? Pull as much good feeling and pure love as you can into this picture.

To return, to come back, pull your attention back to the space between your parallel hands. Once you are back between your hands, put your fingertips and wrists back together. Pull your open-prayer diamond-shaped space back to the area in front of your chest.

Now take your self and press it back into your body by turning each of your palms toward your chest and pushing them into your chest. Welcome back.

You are free to come and go at will using the methods in this chapter. Always return as described in this exercise until you understand what is involved in leaving for good, as is discussed further in Volume Three of this series.

Chapter 13

Initiating the Vision

Even if some stars are smaller than others,
they all shine with a single light.
—St. Makarios the Great of Egypt,
MAKARIAN HOMILIES III

Your higher vision is the key, the guide, the magician, unlocking the door to realities beyond all you think you know. Learn to *see*. Initiate your vision. *See* your way through all your deaths.

See Beyond the Material Plane

We have explained that every major transition, every major ending, is a death. Your notion of dying is itself in transition as you read this. Dying is beginning to look like seeing more than ever before seen, like enlightenment. (The basic practices discussed in Part II of this volume are foundational or key practices of enlightenment regarding light.)

Becoming lighter, understanding the relationship between

the sensations of a high pure form of love and a high pure form of light, romancing (getting close to) the light and clarifying the light, are all exercises for the inner eye. These train your ability to see far beyond the material plane. You will remember engaging in these practices of enlightenment when you find yourself amidst even your most profound changes and even the most disorienting phases of your most advanced transitional deaths.

This is why it is helpful to make some memorable connection with the light now, at this stage of your life, before you are deep into another transition, another ending or another death. It is time, therefore, to initiate your vision, to welcome your new eyes.

Exercise 13.1: Initiating the Vision

Stand if you can. Otherwise, imagine that you are standing. Place your left hand on top of your head. Place your right hand over your heart. (Or imagine that you are doing these things.) Now close your eyes in order to imagine this ceremony.

You stand at the center of a circle of unidentifiable beings, each made of a very beautiful light. These beings are dignitaries of some sort. After a long period of silence, the beings step forward to you, closing their circle in around you. One by one, the beings place their right hands on top of your left hand, which you still hold atop your head. Each being places a right hand atop the hand placed there by the previous being.

One by one, with each hand being placed, you feel and see a bolt of cool and soothing light race into you from the hands—into the top of your head, down your back along your spine and then up the front of you to your heart. The energy grows; the light grows. It becomes quite intense. For a moment, you feel you are being electrocuted, but then you tell yourself that this series of energy surges is too lovely to be an electrocution.

You start to vibrate, to shake. Imagine this or actually do this. Your eyes are still closed. The dignitaries fade away as you begin to shake quite hard. Shake. Open your eyes. Feel that the world looks somehow different.

Exercise 13.2: Raising the Eyes

Close your eyes. Become as aware as you can of all that your eyes feel. Notice that it seems that there are sensations around and even in your eyeballs. These sensations take many forms and can be quite faint. Continue to detect these sensations.

Open your eyes. Fix your gaze on something in your visual field. As you look at this object of your gaze, feel again the sensations around and even in your eyeballs. Feel that seeing this object is, in a way, forming a relationship with your eyeballs, causing an exchange of energy with them.

Now close your eyes and imagine that you are still seeing the object of your gaze. Put this object in your forehead. Feel that seeing this object is exchanging information with it. As you do this, see the object turn to light. Feel your forehead turn to light. Stay with this sensation for several minutes.

Now open your eyes.

Having initiated your vision, you will begin to see more. At first you will barely notice your enhanced vision. Eventually you will rely on it more than your biological vision.

Chapter 14

LEAP Level Two: Quickening for Frequency Shifting

Mere man, his days are numbered;
whatever he may do, he is but the wind.
—Epic of Gilgamesh,
Old Babylonian Version,
YALE TABLET IV

As you move out of your old reality, your old relationship, your old home, your old job, your old youth, your old physical existence, something about you always changes form. You shift to a new arrangement of your consciousness matrix. You shift to a new dimension of your self.

Rearrange Your Consciousness Matrix

Such a shift involves what can be described as a *rearrangement of your consciousness matrix*, or a change in the frequency at which your consciousness matrix vibrates. Ideally, you quicken. As with evaporating water, increasing the motion, the speed of the molecules or of the essence, increases the fluidity or possibility of great change. Such an increase in speed of vibration is indeed a "quickening." This quickening is indeed a great LEAP.

Exercise 14.1: Speeding Up as Frequency Shifting

Lie still with your eyes closed. Imagine that you are on some kind of train that has been stopped for quite some time. Now imagine that this train is slowly entering into motion.

From being entirely still, you begin to move ever so slowly, not even a few miles per hour. Then you move a few miles per hour faster . . . and then a little faster . . . then faster. Now you are moving at freeway speed, as though you were driving on the freeway, whatever this may be for you. Now faster. Now you are moving faster than you have ever driven a car (if you have ever driven a car).

Now you are moving even faster than that, maybe at the speed of the fastest bullet train. Now you are moving at the speed of the fastest Concorde jet. Now you are moving at an even faster speed, faster than the fastest jet, however this speed feels to your imagination. Now you are hurtling through space at the fastest speed you can imagine. Feel yourself speeding up beyond any speed you have ever before imagined.

Note that the train you were in has dropped away from you now but that you are still hurtling through space, retaining your body. There are no wheels moving you; no engines are moving you. You, yourself, are moving you—every atom of your body is propelling you through space. You are moving very fast. Steadily increase your speed as you enter the next exercise. Keep your eyes closed.

Exercise 14.2: Quickening

Continue with closed eyes. Now you are moving far more rapidly. You can feel each of your atoms vibrate. Everything in you seems to be shaking, vibrating.

You are speeding up, quickening. Like water boiling . . . at a certain point, the speed of that boil vaporizes the water. Now you vaporize. Your particles quicken. You do not disappear, you do not die; you simply vaporize. Your body evaporates.

You vaporize, thinking that this could be the end—the end of your consciousness, the end of your awareness. However, as you vaporize, tell yourself to stay conscious. Say, "Remain conscious." Do not let go of your awareness.

Finish vaporizing. Keep on quickening. You are moving ever more rapidly now. You have no physical shape. Now you move as racing vapor. You remain conscious.

It may be hard to imagine vapor moving so quickly, because we tend to think of solid objects and solid bodies moving quickly, hurtling through space. Nevertheless, picture yourself as a vaporous cloud hurtling through space at what you imagine to be the speed of light, and then faster than the speed of light, and then faster than that, and then quicker and quicker. Keep going at this astounding pace, becoming increasingly vaporous. Keep going, keep quickening.

Freeze. Keep your eyes closed.

You are suspended in space, far, far out of your body. Are you breathless? Float and swim and poke around out there as if you had a body. You are still conscious. Examine what you are now. Get to know your consciousness while it is way out there. Study your consciousness for quite a while.

Now clap your hands and return to your physical body. Open your eyes.

Quicken Your Vibration

With an understanding of, a shift in awareness regarding your consciousness, you can learn to raise, to quicken its vibration. In so doing, you increase the energy you have available to you as you prepare to make a major change in your life, in your reality, in your consciousness. You quicken for your LEAP into great change. As you quicken, you raise toward the frequency of high light, which fuels your passage into higher realms of being, which energizes your ascension.

Quickening can be a subtle transition or quite abrupt. Do not be surprised if you feel a rush of energy as your awareness of frequency raises its frequency in order to be aware of so much more.

PART III

HOW TO DETACH

Part III of this book looks at the pervasive and too oft cumbersome attachment to reality that hinders the ease of a change, transition, death—whether a living death or a physical death. Knowing what it means to detach and how to detach from attachments in life is central to structuring one's mastery of death technologies and all relevant keys and LEAPs.

Chapter 15

Detecting the Network of Cords

The will has its loathings and yearnings . . .
—QI BO
CLASSIC OF THE SPIRITUAL AXIS (LING SHU) NEI JING

Y ou create, by existing, a complex web of energy circuits. These circuits flow through and wear pathways into your nervous system, which is a physical extension of your consciousness matrix (and vice versa). These energy circuits also extend far past your nervous system.

You release electrical waves and nets from your biological system. You release biochemical, intellectual, emotional and other more abstract forms of energy into the atmosphere around you. You also tie into electrical and other energy networks above, beyond, outside your own biological and consciousness systems. In fact, you are so tied into your own and other external networks, that you are, in a sense, merged with them. Better stated, you may allow yourself to become *sub*merged in them. You may tend to confuse your consciousness matrix with them.

But you are neither your own nor the external networks you connect to. You are something else—*you.*

Key to the process of detaching clearly is unraveling your identity—disentangling yourself from your (and other people's) attachments to what feels to be your reality, your life. The entangling of one's own reality with attachments of self and others can run so very deep that the disentangling process itself can feel like dying.

Unravel Your Cords

The overlap of your consciousness matrix with your own and others' external energy fields is best understood in terms of inter-personal relationships (which is but one form of this overlap). Your energy field overlaps with the energy fields of the people around you. You come into contact with other people's energy fields and establish relationships or connections with them.

Even when you think you are not involved, you have "hooked up" with other people. You project bits of your reality onto them. You also internalize, take in and live out, feel other people's experiences, their realities, and may assume that some pieces of them are your own. In time, your emotional patterns, your psychological states, your energy patterns, your neurologi-cal patterns, your physical health and your social interactions reflect not just your own conditions and your own states of mind and body but those of the people you have internalized or taken in—and those of the population and even the species you are a member of.

This connection with the people and the world around you is natural. It is, however, important to become as conscious as pos-sible of the energetic effects of such connection or attaching—

or *cording.* It is important to understand, identify and be able to unravel these cords in order to know where you are on your own life path (and where you are in your own various cycles of endings and beginnings).

Especially when it comes to the death of a behavior, of a way of life, or of a physical body, it is important to make:

- the distinction between self and others
- the distinction between self and what may appear to be self but is not self

These distinctions are key. They are essential in determining whether or not it is your time to enter any major transition or to physically die. Always with regard to other persons with whom you are involved or with regard to other attachment factors, ask:

- Am I the one who needs to change, or is it someone else?
- Am I the one who needs to die, or is it someone else?
- Am I the one who needs to die this death this way, or is this someone else?

Sometimes you die, go into transition (including becoming mentally or physically ill), for other people who need to. You cannot determine for someone else whether or not he or she is ready to change or die. That person has to decide for him or her self. You can, however, *decide for yourself whether what you are feeling (the push to change or to end a feeling, a behavior, a relationship, a way of life—the push to die) is your own or someone else's.* This is a very important distinction. Far too frequently, individuals get distracted, stressed, upset or sick, or they die while taking on and experiencing someone else's problems and deaths without realizing they have done so.

Source the Feelings

Perhaps you wake up one morning feeling ill at ease, but you find no reason to feel so. Turn your perception of this feeling around, away from your self, and say, "I don't feel this way. Who (or *what*) in my world, in my life, has a reason to feel (or appear to seem) this way?" It is very important to do this kind of examination of your feelings. This is part of knowing yourself and detecting the network of cords, the web that entangles you. You will benefit by knowing the difference between your own and other people's networks.

If you are dangerously entangled in your own network, you can unravel all or some of it. If you are overidentifying with someone else's network, you can exit all or part of it without doing the work of unraveling for that person.

Exercise 15.1: Sourcing Feelings

Note an uncomfortable emotion you have experienced, even momentarily, sometime recently. Source these feelings.

Ask yourself, "Is this my emotion? Are these my feelings?" Run down the list of your relationships: "How do I feel about my family? Is there anyone I'm close to who hasn't felt right lately? Is anyone worrying me?" Take each person separately and ask yourself why he or she may be worrying you.

Next look at how you have been feeling. Have you been sleeping well? How are your finances? How is your marriage, if you have one? How is your primary relationship, if you have one? Deliberately name one person you are closest to and say, "Jim. How is Jim feeling?

Does Jim feel to me as if Jim's mind is all clear?"

Consider a few other of the more memorable emotions you have experienced recently. Source these feelings as well: "Is this my feeling, or someone else's?"

Sourcing feelings is key here. Sourcing feelings is a diagnostic skill and a survival skill. When you take on (personally experience some or all of) someone else's illness or someone else's dying, in a way you are serving the role of doctor, diagnosing what is wrong with the other person. This is sensitive of you—it enables you to feel empathy for and possibly even help that person. But you need not take the illness or problem or death on; you just are diagnosing what he or she has taken on.

Identification Diagnosis

Let's call this taking on or becoming deeply aware of someone else's problem *identification diagnosis*. With identification diagnosis, you can allow yourself the intuitive awareness of what someone else's condition would be like for you. You actually do this sort of identifying all the time. But *you must do this as consciously as possible.* Identify consciously the energetic condition, and as you do so, identify *whose condition it actually is*—its source. Without being very conscious during your ongoing identification diagnoses, you risk taking on someone else's disease and despair.

Once you have separated out the conditions of others from your own condition and seen your own mix of conditions and those mixes of conditions affecting, emanating from the people in your life, you can move ahead with clarity. *You can follow*

your own life stream, clearing your path of others' issues. This
sourcing is a continuous process.

It is important here to underscore the fact that we are all
part of the larger system. That which affects our children, our
spouses, our friends, members of our community, somebody on
the other side of the globe or even the cosmos, affects us.
Nevertheless, we have to *draw boundaries* when making major
determinations about the steps in our lives that we must take
and the deaths we ourselves must undergo.

Die your own deaths. Leave others to do their own dying. Or if
you are truly certain you wish to, know clearly that you have made
a choice to undergo someone else's process, transition, ending, and
even someone else's death. (There is a big difference between
being supportive and guiding during another person's troubles or
dying processes, and allowing ourselves to personally absorb and
take on the pain and suffering we think we see, hear and feel.)

This is easy to say. Yet it is quite difficult to separate our
fates from the fate of the surrounding world.

Exercise 15.2: Seeing the Larger Manipulation

*Think of your body as a vehicle. Think of your life as the road
your vehicle is traveling on. Drive along for many minutes. Think
of yourself as the driver. Sightsee memories of your life along the side
of the road.*

*While you drive, consider this: In the cosmic order of things,
there are far larger relationships than the relationship between yourself and your vehicle, and between your vehicle and your life path or
road. There are many strings or cords attached to your self, to you
the driver. In fact, as a driver, you may tend more to be somewhat
of a marionette, with other forces far greater than you pulling your*

strings, driving you, at least at times. You are not always in control.

Feel yourself driving along. Imagine that there are strings attached to your hands, your eyelids, your shoulders, your lips. Imagine cords attached to your chest, pulling it in and out, causing you to breathe. Generate the sensation that you are not driving your vehicle, that you yourself are being operated. Imagine for a moment that you are a puppet on strings. Now drive along this way.

See the memories you drive by as memories that are also on puppet strings. Try to look beyond. Try to imagine or see who all have been pulling on those strings.

It is most necessary to examine the strings, the cords connecting us to things and people around us. Inasmuch as we have permitted these cordings, these attachments, we can consciously decide whether we want to clear their influence upon us once we identify them. We can even cut these strings, these cords, if we really wish to.

Exercise 15.3: Listing Your Cords

This exercise is helped by using pen and paper—colored pens and large paper if you have them. This is a brainstorming process, designed to help you visualize or see some of the attachments or cords you have formed in this lifetime.

This process will take your blindfold off. It will take the lock off the door to your self-awareness. The process will snowball. For every attachment or cord you identify, there will be at least one if not several other cords that will come to your mind. Over time, even after this exercise, other cords will surface into your consciousness.

Lifting the obvious cords by listing them allows the more hidden or implicit cords to float to the surface of your consciousness. (This is a bit like the way bathtub toys float to the surface of the bath water when the other floating toys on top of them are removed.) As you continue looking for cords in your life, you will begin to see them as if they were a web of strings, tying you to the world around you.

Now begin to list every cord that comes to mind—every connection you have in your life. Try to find attachments in each of the attachment categories below. Remember, there are no right or wrong categories or answers here. If you are using pen and paper, list each of the categories below with space to write between them. Recognize that these categories overlap. They are listed separately to stimulate your brainstorming. You can also list your own categories, or leave out categories altogether.

You are listing cords. If you are writing your list onto paper, try using a different color pen for each attachment category. Once you have listed each category, list as many cords as you can think of in each of these categories.

Attachment categories can include:

1. *Practical Attachment Cordings*
    - 1a. *Time/schedule/temporal cords*
    - 1b. *Convenience/distance cords*
    - 1c. *Other practical-issue cords*
2. *Physical Attachment Cordings*
    - 2a. *Thing/object cords*
    - 2b. *Location/setting cords*
    - 2c. *Weather cords*
    - 2d. *Other physical-issue cords*
3. *Interpersonal Attachment Cordings*
    - 3a. *Interaction/relationship cords*
    - 3b. *Social-contact cords*

3c. *Psychological cords*

3d. *Energetic cords*

3e. *Other interpersonal-issue cords*

4. *Biochemical and Chemical Attachment Cordings*

    4a. *Nutritional cords*

    4b. *Drug and alcohol cords*

    4c. *Environmental-exposure cords*

    4d. *Other biochemical/chemical cords*

5. *Larger Social Environment Cords*

    5a. *Cultural cords*

    5b. *Political cords*

    5c. *Media/music/television/radio cords*

6. *Spiritual Cords*

    6a. *Need for/meaning-in-life cords*

    6b. *Need for/belief-system cords*

7. *Other Categories of Cords You May Think Of*

Do not force yourself to define cords right now, or to fit precisely into any of the above categories. Just list anything that comes to your mind, anything that you think of as being part of your life as you decide for yourself what the above attachment categories suggest to you. Again, there are no right or wrong answers here.

Exercise 15.4: Adding Cords to Your List

Review the list you created in Exercise 15.3. Now add at least five more cords in each category.

If this is difficult, invent attachment cordings or subcategories of these. You may want to think in terms of primary (very obvious or explicit), secondary (less obvious, less explicit) and tertiary (very hidden or implicit) cords. For example, a man in love with a woman may be attached to—corded to—the physical body of the woman he is in love with. A secondary cord for him might be the sound of her voice. A tertiary or very subtle cord for him might be something that reminds him of either a primary or secondary cord (such as an old photograph of her or a piece of music they listened to together five years ago).

You may want to expand the list you created in Exercise 15.3 by adding columns to it this way:

	Primary Cords	Secondary Cords	Tertiary Cords
Practical Cords	↓	↓	↓
Physical Cords			
Interpersonal Cords			
Etc.			

However you go about your brainstorming, be sure to write down anything that comes into your mind, no matter how trivial or out of place it may seem. Any association at all that comes to your mind is ripe material for this cord chart. Do not try to make sense out of everything that comes to your mind. Do not force yourself into cord categories. Do not force yourself to make complete sense. Just let it all come into your awareness and write it all down. Write as quickly as you can without trying to be neat. You can clean up your list and organize it later, even copy it over if you wish.

Once you have listed everything you can think of, draw a box or circle around each individual cord, whether that cord is minor or major to you—whether it's a primary, secondary or tertiary cord. Do this even with the cords that seem questionable, trivial, out of order or illogical to you.

Exercise 15.5: Connecting Your Cords to Form Patterns

Now examine all of your cords—do you feel that any of them are connected? If so, connect them; draw a line between these cords. Some connections will seem logical; others will seem to make no sense at all.

Think about a connection you found. Some connections will appear to be rituals, habit patterns and even pattern addictions. For example, at six o'clock Friday (a time cord), a person who ends the work week at this point in time may regularly go to a particular bar (an environmental cord), where she or he may meet various friends and a date (social and interpersonal cords), upon which he or she may feel like "partying" (a psychological cord) and may proceed to eat a large amount of salty nuts and potato chips instead of a real dinner because she or he is hungry but too lazy to eat right (a nutritional cord). And after all that salt, she or he may be so thirsty that she or he has far more alcohol to drink than he or she means to (a drug and alcohol cord), which she or he actually does quite regularly.

This is a fairly obvious cord network or attachment pattern. Note that this particular cord network is a habit pattern and may be part of a more serious pattern addiction to alcohol.

Other attachment patterns (and even addictions to these patterns of attachment) may be less clear, but any patterns that come to mind should be recorded. [Pattern addiction was discussed in Volume One of this series.] Your cord networks are pieces of your web. Here in this web of attachments, your patterning and deep-seated pattern addictions can lurk.

Continue to map out relations between the various cords you have listed. Observe the patterns that emerge. The charts at the end of this chapter are actually simple, partial excerpts of maps of several different individuals' cord networks [see Figures 15.1–15.6]. Notice the similarities and differences in these and your own charts.

Exercise 15.6: Planning Future Cord Observations

Your cord chart should be reconstructed regularly. Add to your first chart daily for a week. Make a new cord chart each week for several weeks, incorporating everything from your old cord chart and pushing yourself to add new details. Then, for the next several months, make a new cord chart once a month. Then shift to two or three times a year.

This will provide you with an amazing journey into your behavior and your web of attachments, and a new level of awareness about yourself. You will begin to see the web you weave, not just on paper, but in the atmosphere around you. This is a most fascinating process.

Whenever you find connections between attachments, cords and more attachments, return to your chart or write a new chart in your mind, drawing lines to demonstrate your newly identified connections. This mapping process will reveal significant and, with practice, astounding information about your most obvious and your most subtle emotional, behavioral and energetic patterns.

As noted above, sample attachment cording charts are found in Figures 15.1–15.6. These are reduced in terms of number of categories due to space limitations here. Note how some of these abbreviated charts emphasize the attachment of cords directly to feelings about attachments rather than to objects of attachments. This is acceptable. Many of us are more attached to our emotions about things and people than we are to these things and people. In fact, if you think about it, all your attachment is actually attachment to your feelings about or perceptions of that to which you think you are attached.

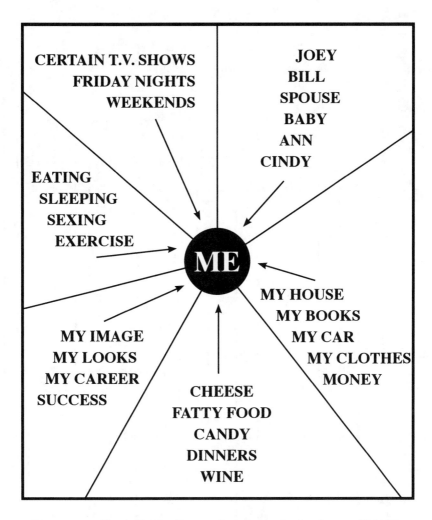

Figure 15.1. An individual's attachments to basic pieces of his life.

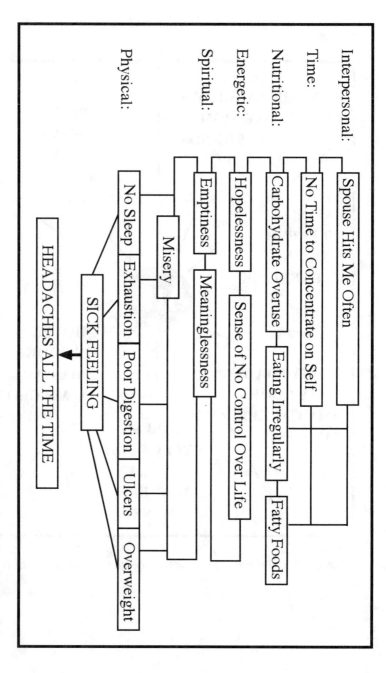

Figure 15.2. Simplified cord network. Drawn by a woman who has chronic migraine headaches and who is living with domestic violence.

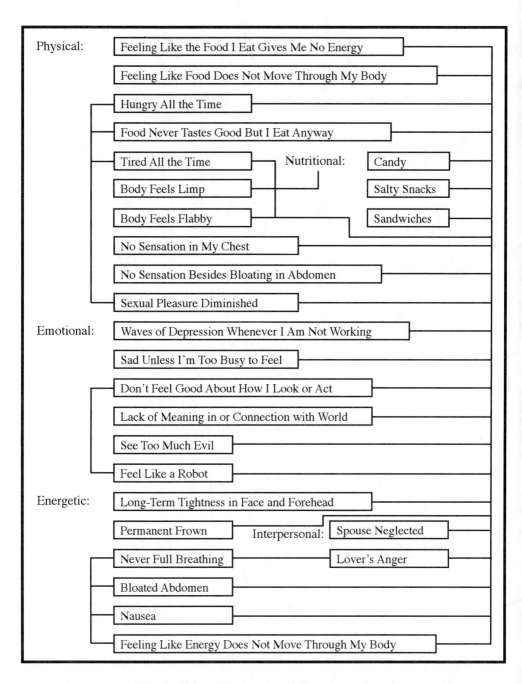

Figure 15.3. Simplified web of life of individual suffering from depression, chronic fatigue and overweight.

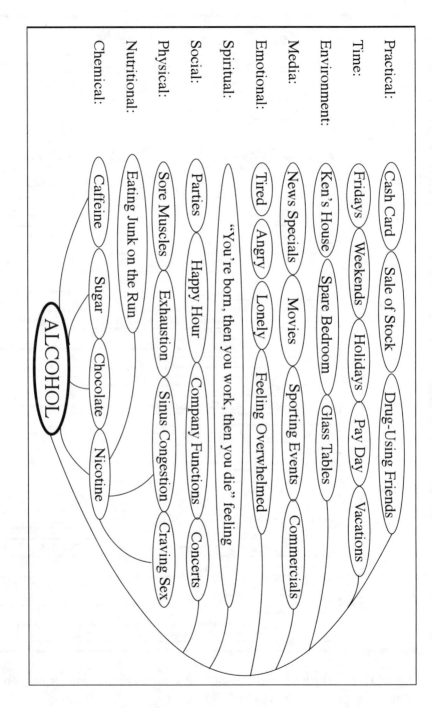

Figure 15.4. Habit pattern of man addicted to alcohol.

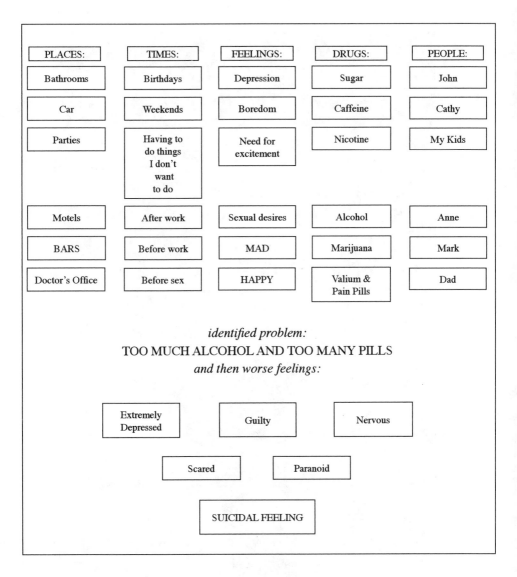

Figure 15.5. Partial attachment chart of suicidal woman (woman claims each item is attached to every other item).

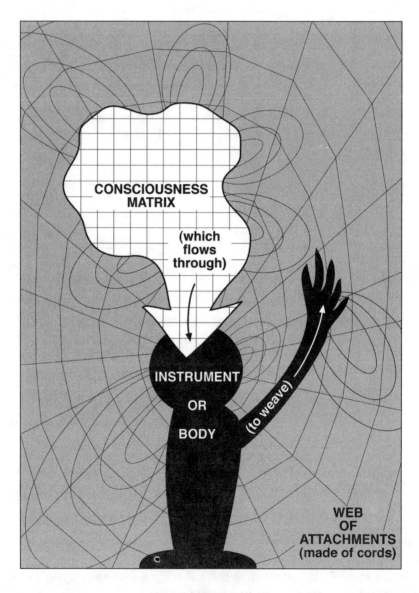

Figure 15.6. Depiction of the web of attachment woven out of cords.

Chapter 16

Releasing Attachments

So before we die we should try to free ourselves of attachment to all our possessions, friends, and loved ones.

—Sogyal Rinpoche,
THE TIBETAN BOOK OF LIVING AND DYING

Many people living in the material plane report that their attachments to—their connections to, desires for, urges or cravings for—the feelings and objects to which and persons to whom they are corded, are overwhelming. People become so very addicted to their realities that they cling to them even as these realities may be sinking like drowning ships. If you are overwhelmingly attached, if you are finding it very difficult or painful to transform or leave situations such as a troubled marriage, an addiction to a drug or a dying body, it is most likely that you are addictively corded. Your conscious mind is driven by a powerful and frequently *subconscious addiction to the attachment patterns* you have formed around the persons, objects, feelings and components of your pattern addiction. Indeed, pattern addiction runs deep and is easily fallen into given that we are coded to develop pattern addictions.

You are not alone. Most individuals experience such pattern addictions. In fact, all beings living in the physical world experience some degree of addiction to their material-plane realities, as suggested in Figures 3.1 and 15.6.

Seeing Attachments

Many individuals feel that they lose control of their wills during their cravings for the objects of their attachments (people, behaviors, things, emotions, sensations and so on). They fall prey to their pattern addictions. They find that their addictions to their patterns of attachment actually commandeer their will powers. In the face of this tendency we all share, the ability to detach is essential.

To master detachment and to detach when you need to, you must learn that *it is possible to live through your longings and cravings for these objects of your attachment without responding to them addictively: habitually, impulsively, compulsively.* But in order to learn how to do this, you must learn to face your habits, compulsions, longings and cravings head-on. "Head-on" here means to really know it, to feel it, to really identify it.

Sometimes fear of the power of a longing or of any sort of desire, urge or craving, leads people to try to avoid constructive concentration on that longing, desire, urge or craving. This is a mistake. Only a clear look at your intense pattern addictions and attachments can enable you to break them. Only a clear look at your addictions and attachments to your reality can enable you to release these attachments—to change your reality, to die out of your reality with grace and increased power.

Consider the experience that a drug- or alcohol-addicted individual undergoes when craving drugs. This craving is a problem of severe physical and emotional attachment. The tendency is to avoid looking the craving in the face. For the drug- or alcohol-addicted person to bring this craving—this intense attachment—into focus, he or she must learn to ask him- or herself, "What of me is craving the drug or alcohol? What part of my body is feeling this craving? Exactly where is this part of my body? Can I give it a feeling to make myself more aware of it? What is the shape of this feeling? Its size? Its temperature? Can a color be attributed to this area?" By assigning characteristics to the intense attachment, this attachment becomes more visible to you. You begin to see it with your inner eye. Your higher vision is further refined.

Whatever attachment you are examining, whether it be one of drug addiction, one of a strong relationship or one of some other type of attachment, you can benefit by giving this attachment flags or characteristics. Keep in mind that many messages from your body and mind go unnoticed by you. Learning to answer the above questions about the characteristics of your attachment can teach you to focus on, to pay attention to what you are actually feeling. Seeking the answers to such questions about the perceived location, size, shape, temperature and color of your attachments generates in you a somewhat meditative state. Your concentration focuses more and more precisely when you try to visualize these characteristics. You visualize, you know, you recognize these places where your cords with the external world are attached.

Exercise 16.1: Seeing Points of Attachment

Think of an object or a person to whom you feel connected in any way. This can be a comfortable or an uncomfortable connection, or both. Concentrate on that object or person for a few minutes.

As you concentrate, concentrate on any physical sensations you may be experiencing. Is there a particular part of your body that you are somewhat more aware of while you concentrate on the object or person you have selected?

Identify this part of your body, no matter how large or small. Make this part of your body the center of your focus, no matter how sure or unsure you are that it is this particular part of your body that is responding to your concentration on the object or person you have selected.

Describe this part of your body to yourself. Notice how you choose to describe it. Push your mind to come up with a very detailed description of the part of your body you have identified with your connection to the object or person you have chosen. Invent details if you need to stimulate your detailing.

Feel that this part of your body is one of the places where a cord between you and that to which you are connected is attached. Create an image of this cord attaching to the part of the body you are detailing. Attach the other end of the cord to the object or person to which you are connected. Study this cord. Study the points of attachment. Are they soft touches, strong anchors, deep roots or piercing hooks?

Learn to Visualize Cords

Practice visualizing your cord network. This is a most useful imagery technique. Imagery techniques are tools of focus. Visual imagery involves using the mind to picture—or to give a picture to—what is going on inside your body and in the space around your body. Individuals who practice visualization can learn to direct increasing levels of concentration to special locations or conditions in their brains, in their bodies and in the space around their bodies. By visualizing what is going on inside your body, your psyche reaches into your soma (your mind reaches into your body) consciously and with a purpose. When you practice visual imagery, you achieve a greater degree of conscious control over your mental and physical health.

In the treatment of a particular health problem—whether that problem is biological or behavioral (the two are often related)—imagery techniques can be tailored to the specific problem being addressed. Visual imagery is a process that reveals how the body and mind are related to each other. The first step in the healing process is to "see" the problem—to go inside the mind and body, and take a good look at what is taking place, what may not be going well, what may be going wrong. When the health problem is distinctly physical, this step is relatively easy. Cellular and other biological activity can be easily visualized. For example, a person suffering from cancer can be helped to "see" what is happening in his body by showing him slides of white cells attacking cancer cells and x-rays showing the location and shape of the growths in his body.

Visualizing is not always this straightforward. It is one thing to form a rather accurate image of a tumor in the mind after looking at x-rays; it is another to "see" the subtle energy patterns that might have caused that cancerous growth. In addition to the fact that energy patterns that affect one's health are subtle and invisible, many psychological conditions have no one distinct and literal physical location to which they can be linked.

When a person is suffering emotionally, there may be no distinct (or readily perceivable) biological indication of this. There may be no growths in the body to x-ray. White cells may not be attacking a tumor. Yet over time, troubled energetic patterns may move from emotional discomfort to physical disease.

This shift from subtle energy patterning down into emotional energy patterning and then down into physical energy patterning is a downward shift—or *descension*—in density. [Refer to Figure 8.1 for a reminder of the realms of density.] While such a descension is not always a disease process, it must be monitored carefully. The energetic cords, the subtle and then emotional attachment patterns we form, can eventually become physical energy patterns.

Identify, really know and then release (let die) problematic cords that may drag you—or your patterning—downward in density before these cords become increasingly problematic, damaging or dangerous.

Change or Eliminate the Cord

Individuals experiencing attachments experience their cordings in myriad ways, unconscious and conscious. Some have vague or intense physical sensations of pain or pleasure or tightness or warmth. Others have vague, almost unnoticeable hints of these cordings, perhaps tied into free-floating anxieties. It is useful to pay close attention to even the most minor sensations and imaginings in order to get a continuous reading on the presence and degree of cording. With practice, you will see more and more of the cords with which you weave your web. With practice, you will notice the network of cords forming between you and even someone you have just met. You will begin to see the webs you and others weave everywhere.

Once the cord or cord network is even vaguely visualized, the image of the cord or cord network can be changed: reduced, rearranged, manipulated, destroyed or replaced with a more desirable picture. This is done by first imagining and visualizing a particular cord or set of cords, and then by creating a tool with which to resculpt or operate, to do *energetic surgery* on this imagery of attachment.

Among the tools that are applicable to this energetic surgery technique are visualizations of beams of light resembling lasers, of balls of light that work like explosive bombs or absorbent sponges, of chains or ropes that tie up the cords, of knives or saws that cut the cords, of paintbrushes or crayons that redraw the cords, and of hands that reach into the attachment picture and operate on the cords. Washing away the cords with luminous soapsuds that give off beautiful light can be an uplifting process. You can also see each cord as an energy string to be unraveled.

With practice, this front-line—highly literal, although seemingly imaginary—confrontation with your attachment cords can be achieved each time you experience a problem of attachment. Cords can be clearly pictured and then operated on by the imagination, the inner surgeon. In so doing, you can gain control over even the most powerful attachments.

This sort of visual imagery focuses your concentration on the experience of attachment in a way that allows you to *be in command of your attachment behavior*, rather than being subservient to it. Sometimes, when your attachment is described in words, any problem associated with it seems intractable. Adding pictures to thinking helps you to be free from the confines of verbal thought and gain power over attachment. The multitude of attachments and the knotty web of their cords that entangle and overwhelm you, can be encapsulated into a single picture, a picture free of words, names or labels. Imagery reduces complicated words to simple, powerful pictures.

Exercise 16.2: Operating on Your Attachment Cords

In order to do this exercise, you will need a peaceful, quiet place where you will be comfortable and will not be disturbed. You may want paper and a set of colored markers.

You might want to have yourself or a friend record, in his or her voice, this exercise for you. Or you might just want to have someone read this exercise aloud to you. Either way, this exercise should be read very slowly, in a very steady, calm voice. Once you have decided how to hear this exercise, relax, listen and concentrate on these words.

Make yourself comfortable. Sit or lie in a comfortable position. If your legs are crossed or bent and you think you will begin to get cramps, stretch them out now. Find a position that you can be relaxed in for a long period of time.

Close your eyes. Breathe slowly. Try to stay awake during this exercise, but do not be concerned about dozing off or tuning out. If you do doze off, pay attention to where you start drifting. It is helpful to see where in this exercise you might tune out, if you do. Repeat the exercise if you do doze off.

Now think of a problematic, a difficult or a challenging attachment you have experienced or are presently experiencing in your life. This can be a connection to an object or a physical thing, or to a person you have had or still have in your reality, one who is perhaps wonderful but hard to let change, or sad, or over. This can also be a drug or other addiction. Stay with this attachment for this exercise.

Do not answer out loud the questions asked of you in this exercise. Try to think without words. Try to think in pictures in your mind. Try to see the answer. Where you cannot see it, hear or taste or smell or feel the answer. When you have no answer, remember to imagine—just make up an answer. Imagining and imaging are very similar processes, and each can supplement the other.

Continue with closed eyes. Again, think of this problematic attachment. Think of one of the last times you felt this attachment. Make this last time the present, even if it is in the past. Where are you, what is your geographical and physical location, as you feel this attachment? See yourself there.

Imagine that you are a filmmaker. Take an invisible movie camera into your hands. You are making a film about this attachment of yours. It will be a slow-motion movie. First you are setting the stage: See the place where you think you last felt this attachment. Move the camera slowly around the room or the car or the building or the beach or wherever your place is. Remember to do this with your eyes closed, because you are looking at a place that is in your memory.

Try to see through the camera lens. See the details: the colors of the walls, if there are walls; the colors that you would see around you; whether the place is messy or neat, orderly or chaotic. If you are indoors, what is hanging on the walls? What furniture is there? Try to feel and see in detail what the place is like. Sometimes your mind remembers details that do not easily come back to you when you consciously try to remember. There might be cracks in the wall, or ants in the corner, or spilled garbage somewhere. These will appear in your movie. Where your memory stops, let your imagination give you whatever details you want to fill in.

These things are there in your memory bank. The more relaxed you are, the more of these little pieces of the whole picture, the more bits of information about your attachment network you will see. There are no people on your stage yet. And remember, everything is in slow motion.

The next assignment for you, the filmmaker, is to set the time of day for this particular memory of this particular attachment. Look through the camera lens at the sky to see the time of day, or through the window, or at the clock on the wall. Show yourself what time of day it is. If you cannot remember, just pick a time.

So now you know the time of day. What is the air temperature? Are you warm or cold or neutral? If you are outside, do you know what the weather is like? If you are inside, what weather do you see through the window? If you cannot remember, pick a weather, pick a temperature, whatever comes to mind.

Now start adding people, if there are people involved in this attachment, to this scene. See them arrive at this place. If there are no people involved in this attachment, you will not add people to this scene. Do not add yourself yet. Invent people to be present if you wish to.

If there are people in this place, turn your movie camera on each of these people and get some close-up looks at their faces. Note your feelings as you see them through the camera lens. This may be the first time you have ever really looked at some of them. Try to see what these people look like. Make up details if you cannot remember any. If there is just one person, get a close look at that one person's face. Look closely at the person or the people. See what they are wearing, how they walk, how they sit, how their faces look.

Now it is time to look at yourself. Put yourself into the scene. Look at yourself more closely than you have ever looked before. You may have to pull the camera up to the ceiling and look down on yourself to see how you looked during this particular experience of your attachment. What state or states of mind, feelings and emotions do you associate with this attachment? Maybe you are happy or celebrating. Perhaps you are bored. Maybe you are hurt. Maybe you are having other feelings. It is difficult to film states of mind, but use your movie camera. You are the star of your movie.

See your face and body language revealing your state or states of mind. Remember, there are all kinds of possible states of mind, and *many of them can be felt at the same time. Let yourself look through your camera lens at those states of mind that you are experiencing. If you cannot remember your state of mind with regard to this attachment of yours, just make it up. If you like, try some states of mind on for size, just to see how they feel. While your eyes are closed, make faces showing different states of mind: a happy face, a hurt face, an irritated face, a sad face, a bored face, a tired face. Whatever expression best reminds you of the state of mind you connect with this attachment, settle into that facial expression.*

Now, in your slow-motion movie, step back and look around the room. The people, if any, are there. You are there. You know what kind of day it is. You know what the place looks like. You know how you look. Now identify the particular object or activity or person you are attached to. Swing the camera around so that you focus in on this object of your attachment.

Take your camera for some close-up shots of what it is you are attached to. Now note that you actually have a very unusual camera. As you take these close-up shots, the camera reveals what is usually invisible to you: the camera reveals strings or cords made of something like light running between you and the object of your attachment.

You are seeing many cords between you and the object of your attachment now. You are looking very closely at these fascinating cords. As you look closely, you, the filmmaker, begin to realize that you—yes, you!—are deeply connected to the object of your attachment by these cords. You are more than connected—you are tangled up. You feel very tied, very entangled in a web of cords. You see this web. You see this web as the web of your pattern addiction.

Somehow now the camera falls or dissolves out of your hands. You stretch your fingers out and run your fingertips along these cords, as if you were playing a harp.

Keep fingering these cords. Let your hands become increasingly stiff while you do this, so that you are putting some stress into your efforts. Your hands are feeling the intensity of your relationship to the objects of your attachment.

Remember to keep your eyes closed while you do this exercise. Now imagine or actually stand up and move into this web of cords. Get further tangled in this web. Try to get out by squirming and struggling. See how this seems to make you more entangled.

Feel an increasing degree of tension as you feel more and more trapped. Feel tense, because this is an intense experience. Let your hands and your arms and your shoulders become very tight. Let your trapped body become very tight. Feel an overbearing amount of tension. Still struggle to get out of the web, and still become ever more entangled. Become tense all over.

Finally, you are so entangled that you cannot move.

You want out. Be extremely tight and tense. You desperately want to burst out but are unable to.

Freeze. Stop time. . . .

Stay frozen, tense, trapped, with your eyes still closed. Note what you are feeling most in your body right now. You may feel something, or you may not consciously feel anything. Allow your subconscious to help you know what you are feeling. Let your imagination participate here.

You may be feeling excess salivation: a watery mouth, or a tight jaw, or pain, or sensation in the sinuses or neck or lower back. You may be feeling a throbbing headache, cold or hot rushes, cold or hot patches, numb patches around the body, a feeling of seasickness or excitement, a knot in your stomach, a tightness in your legs, lead in your feet ... or vague pleasure ... or hints of release or relief.

You may be feeling pain or tightness in the heart area. You might find it difficult to breathe. You may want to cry or laugh hysterically. There are so many things you might be feeling: slight prickly sensations at a few points in your body, a tiny itch, a small area of pressure.

Be alert. Look closely, deep inside. Most of the time, we miss noting the sensation of attachment because we are so hooked into our attachments that we run on automatic. We are not in touch with what we are feeling, with where these attachments connect, with the tugs and effects of such connections.

Yet this time you are concentrating on what you are sensing. Pick one or two of your most present feelings and let yourself feel these.

Identify the part or parts of your body that you are most aware of right now. You are definitely aware of something. It may just be the feeling of touching the chair or the floor. But it might be a feeling that has come out of your experience or one of the feelings mentioned a moment ago.

Now pretend that one of your fingers is a colored felt pen. Pick a color, and imagine yourself to be outlining the area of your body that you are most aware of. Outline that part several times. If the area is hot, use a warm color. If it is cold, use a cool color.

Now pretend to color this area in—you may want to use some other colors. If you have a knot in your stomach, draw the knot. If your heart is beating quickly, you might want to use some color that reminds you of a fast pulse, high blood pressure and maybe tension. Everybody sees her or his own colors. You may be feeling other things in this part or some other part of your body. You might be having feelings without knowing which part of the body those feelings are coming from. Try to give those feelings a place in your body.

With your finger, draw one or more cords coming out of this place in your body.

See the cord or cords reaching into the air—see the cord or cords go from this place in your body you have identified to the object of your attachment. See several tangled cords running between you and the object of your attachment. See yourself tangled in these cords.

Now light these cords up, as if they were overheated electric wires. Light these cords up to the brightest, hottest, most intense light possible. Light them up so much that they smoke. Keep overheating these cords with light. Hold. Hold this light now.

Hold . . . until suddenly the cords evaporate, leaving behind only a bit of white smoke.

Realize that you are free of the entanglement and release your tense body. Breathe in, and then, aloud, release a big sigh of relief. Say, "Aaahhh," aloud if you wish.

Very good. You did a great job!

Now with your eyes still closed, do nothing but feel whatever you are feeling.

Open your eyes. Draw a picture (on paper or in your mind) of yourself at your most cord-entangled point during this exercise. Label this picture "Before." Draw/see yourself after the release. Label this picture "After."

Learn to recognize the release of an attachment. Absorb the sensation of *attachment release*. Store this sensation in your memory and refer to it during your transitions, endings and dyings. You will need to recall this sensation time and again. You will need to invoke this sensation in order to bring on the small and large releases you will need to experience in order to move on. The highest release consists of a few simple and rather traditional steps*:

- Say, "Light up": Light the cord or cords up like overheated electrical wires.
- Say, "Deconstruct": See these cords vaporize or dissolve.
- Say, "Transmute to the highest light": See the debris—what remains—turned to the highest, purest light.

Exercise 16.3: Deconstructing and Transmuting Cords

Close your eyes. Open your mind's eye. Say aloud, "I call upon my inner vision." Now see several cords forming between you and someone or something else—from some points in or on your body to some points in or on an object or person. See the strands of these cords materializing. When the cords are in place, visualize yourself deconstructing them one by one, saying aloud each time:

- *"Light up." (Light the cord up.)*
- *"Deconstruct." (Dissolve the cord.)*
- *"Transmute to the highest light." (Turn what remains to a pure white light.)*

Do this again and again for each cord, and then continue chanting for several minutes: "Light up. Deconstruct. Transmute to the highest light. . . . Light up. Deconstruct. Transmute to the highest light. . . . Light up. Deconstruct. Transmute to the highest light. . . ."

---

* Forms of this process are found in numerous spiritual teachings of diverse origin. Here this form is reframed for the practice of release (specifically death) and transition-related release of one's own and others' attachments to one's life.

LIGHT UP.

DECONSTRUCT.

TRANSMUTE.

CLEAR.

Chapter 17

Clearing Subtle Energy Webs

If one does not understand how the body that he wears came to be, he will perish with it . . .

—Dialogue of the Savior 134:1–22, Nag Hammadi Library

With a refocusing of the eye, you see the web you have woven around you. It is like a very complex spider web stringing outward from you in all directions. Once you become sensitive to your own web and the webs around you, you will find yourself continuously relying upon this knowledge. You can form useful energetically balanced webs if you can see them in the making and influence their construction. You can consciously and with specificity clear yourself of detrimental webs if you can detect their presence.

Use Intuition to Find and Clear Subtle Energy Cords

Everyone uses intuition, but not everyone uses intuition consciously. Using intuition is like listening to very fine, very faint, very distant music.

You can use your intuition to help you see the attachment cords of subtle energy webs. Your intuition is always at work, although it is frequently clouded by biased impressions and blinded by distractions. You are most intuitively aware of the people you know best.

Consider the relationship you may have to a strong mother figure, perhaps your own mother. You have a feel for that person. The music of that person has become a familiar song. Maybe one day, suddenly you feel a few notes in that familiar song change. Perhaps you then say, "I've been thinking about Mother. I'd better call her." You are not necessarily sure why you want to call; you just sense that suddenly her program feels different. There is a little change there. You do not necessarily realize this change consciously, but you call, and you discover that your mother has just been rushed to the hospital. Maybe your mother is elderly and ill, and so this does not entirely surprise you, as this happens with people who have been around a long time. Still, you knew on some level that something different was happening with your mother.

Become aware of how these intuitions work. They are quite subtle. If someone plays you the same song a hundred times and then plays it one more time with only one note changed, you may not notice the difference but you will sense it. If you have walked into a room daily for ten years and that room has never been rearranged until today, and now one pillow has been moved, you may not notice the change, but you will sense it.

Your relationships to subtle energy-formed attachments, or cords, are similar. Sometimes you do not see (in material reality) a shift or change in energy, but you sense it. On some intuitive level, you feel a tug on the cord, or a wriggling, or some other sensation of action there.

Notice this sort of subtle sensation. Perhaps a cord is being fed, fueled, or is being pulled upon, tugged. Ask yourself what this feeling could relate to. Is your energy, including perhaps your health, being sucked on, drained away from you, or altered against your will by another person? Or is someone perhaps demanding something from you, a response from you, a behavior from you, attention from you, attachment from you, pulling on you in some way?

Is this a big or a small matter? Is this a life or death thing? Or is this maybe your own need or insecurity—are you doing the tugging? Give this sensation a label or a name to make it more clear.

Give yourself a particular description of what you sense, even if it may not be quite right. Wait. Adjust the label until a better one comes out. With practice, you will find that you can actually adjust the label until it comes out right.

Detect Subtle Information

Become aware of the subtle changes in your own and others' energy fields. Hear how the music shifts. It takes relaxed and focused concentration to know who you are in the subtle energy communication. Are you the one playing the music? Did you just change a note in the song—or did someone else? This knowing process involves a strong consciousness and an awareness of your relationship to your cord network within the world around you. The stronger your consciousness, the more willing you are to identify with your own consciousness matrix and not someone else's, the more you can count on your intuition to see what is going on in your cord network.

Heighten your awareness by paying close attention to detail. Say you notice a slight shift in the taste in your mouth. Ask yourself, "What about this new taste in my mouth? Do I notice this often, or only when I am not feeling well? Do I notice this right before I get sick to my stomach, or right before something else happens?" There are subtle shifts occurring in your body chemistry at all times. Pay attention to these. Do not force meaning on them; just start noticing them. Notice varying tastes, smells, glimpses of things. Notice faint sounds and their fluctuations, appearances and disappearances. *Notice shifts in what you hear as the background noise.* Are there any overtones, any high sounds you can barely hear at all and rarely pay attention to?

NOTICE MORE.

Exercise 17.1: Higher Hearing

Close your eyes. Listen for sounds that you cannot hear with your ears. Plug your ears—now listen. What do you hear? Imagine that you hear more than you do. Work on this for a while. This form of hearing slips in slowly and becomes sharper with practice.

Examine the Subtle Network

It is easy to pick up some other individual's feelings and mistake them for your own, and then react as if these were your feelings. Sometimes someone surprises you with anger, and although you are not angry, you get mad right back. That person throws a ball of anger at you, and you pick it up and throw it back. Had you just let the ball of anger lie there, there would be no ball game. The ball game is further weaving the web, further fortifying the cords.

After some repeated travel along its cords, the network of cords becomes a powerful pattern. It becomes harder and harder to break out of the loops of networked cords. Physical death offers the most certain erasure of any such strong patterning. However, there are other options. Deeply buried patterns can be recognized and manipulated. Lifestyles can be altered in a pragmatic, multilevel way. Spiritual structure can be developed in order to bring about transcendence. (The steps into or phases of transcendence are described in Volume One.)

These options fall into the realm of energy work. You must learn to work on the energetic level. This is important work, as you can do it regardless of your physical condition or health, and you can do it in the material plane and in other dimensions as well. Think of it this way: You can do energy surgery on yourself whether or not you have a physical body. If your consciousness has developed a problematic consciousness matrix or troubled pattern of energy and information flow, you can use your conscious mind to change your consciousness.

Here the use of *insight imagery* is valuable. Images of networks, webs, cords, patterns of cords—whether entirely imagined, generally intuited or based on experiential information—can be built in the mind's eye. These images, based upon the agreement to see energy that one can make with one's mind, can represent otherwise invisible and inconceivable energetic patterns. Once visualized, these patterns can be worked with, changed and/or eliminated. (More on this sort of energy surgery and further detail regarding the changes that can be made in these patterns can be found in Volume Three.)

Exercise 17.2: Clearing Subtle Webs

Visualize yourself sitting across from someone you know but do not know well. Choose someone with whom you do not have what you consider an intense relationship. Imagine that—for this exercise only and not necessarily in "real" life—you want to disconnect, detach from this person.

Visualize a network of cords connecting you, from various points on your body, to this person, at various points on his or her body. Close your eyes and take some time to see how very intricate even this network is. See that this network is far more intricate than you expected.

Now light up each and every strand of this network. Hold this image a moment. When you hear the word "deconstruct," dissolve all of this network immediately.

DECONSTRUCT.

CLEAR.

You have cleared this piece of subtle energy web.

If you wish to reinstate all or some of this web, do so before you open your eyes, by visualizing this happening and saying, "Reconstruct."

RECONSTRUCT.

Chapter 18

Clearing Social Energy Webs

Here is where love burns with an innocent flame:
the clean desire for death. . . .

—Thomas Merton,
ENTERING THE SILENCE

Now that we have looked at the very subtle network of energy cords, the attachments forming the subtle energy web, let's step back and see what is, by comparison, believed to be the more tangible social or interpersonal energy web. Social energy webs are woven out of behaviors and feelings. We think we see signs of and even think we feel these behaviors and feelings.

While the reality of the social and interpersonal energy web, its network and the specific cords within it are not readily spotted by a novice, they are more easily recognized by any of us after examining the subtle energy interaction level. This examination is important in order to see how living persons cord and attempt to disallow the de-cording process of the dying.

Lies Form Cords

Of course, for the most part, no one claims to cord. Instead, we all lie to each other and ourselves by denying or failing to see the many fibers of our many cordings. Even lies themselves can form cords, usually nonverbally. These are lies about the fact that we are doing cording, lies that cord by tying themselves to the objects of these lies.

Lying takes on new importance here. Lies form cords. Every single lie, whether conscious or not, affects the web. Entire relationships—most relationships, in fact—are built upon lies regarding the cording being done. Entire energy patterns, cord networks between people—friends, colleagues, coworkers, lovers, family members, neighbors—may be (and usually are) built with no discussion of them. Lack of direct communication about the cording being done has become so very common that most people have adjusted to it and do not find this at all unusual.

Even when any sort of communication does occur, it can be inadequate: "I told you to be home by six." "I didn't hear you." "That's your problem. No dinner for you now." "Who cares? I had two milkshakes while I waited for you to pick me up. You never came." "You didn't tell me you needed a ride." This kind of conversation is inadequate in that it does not express the fact that one person was wondering where the other person was and was concerned for her welfare, while that person was hurt that no one came to pick her up. Inadequate communication is taking place when feelings and facts are buried under accusations and counteraccusations. Each of these accusations and counteraccusations forms a particularly nasty cord.

Confusion Forms Cords

Reality is further distorted when communication becomes confused—which, when we take into account the continuous overlooking of cords, is most of the time. So much is not said. So much of what is said has no clear meaning. Even subtle body language—looks in eyes, swallowings of saliva and more—say things we may miss. The scramble is ongoing and becomes the reality for many people. The only consistency in communication is consistent ambiguity. This can be frightening to those corded to each other as they cannot be trusted to be consistently clear. One minute one of them is loving and kind to the other; the next, he or she is threatening and cruel. And then the two people switch roles.

Then the messages are not trustworthy, not clear. The confused communication of one person leads others to become confused communicators in order to cope, compete, survive or just fit in. Confused communication can plant the seeds of deep emotional disturbance in children and adolescents—seeds that may emerge later in adult life as deep neuroses. We see the effects of, the tugs of the cords of confused communication everywhere.

Pain Forms Cords

Lies and broken communication can lead to unexpressed, partially expressed or indirectly expressed pain. When this pain is not fully expressed, the person who has been hurt is likely to develop a grudge. Pain and its grudges form powerful and long-lasting cords.

Many grudges remain unadmitted to others as well as to ourselves. Such a private grudge is a strange thing. It is a stuffed-away, unexpressed emotion that is always unstuffing itself and breaking out in troubled, stiff, cold or angry ways. Grudges develop slowly, when communications continue to fail and the lies, confusion and pain compound. Many children grow up feeling that their siblings or their parents have grudges against them—although no one ever talked about it and nothing was ever done that was hurtful enough to prove that a grudge actually existed.

Some grudges do become public—they are made obvious. A least favored or always blamed member of the family may be the subject of a public family grudge. This person often develops private grudges in response and retaliation to family members' grudges against him or her.

Some hurt takes the tone of a stronger grudge, or revenge: "You hurt me; I'll hurt you back." This is an eye-for-an-eye, tit-for-tat type of hurt. But even more dangerous is hurt that has been buried. Many individuals go through half their lives before discovering and learning to express their buried hurt. Too often buried hurt is directed against oneself before it can be expressed in a healthy way. When this happens, an individual has become entangled in deeply attached cords of pain.

Many people who have buried hurt—hurt they may not even realize they have—express it through cords of secret hurt back. They direct or attach subtle revenges to others who have hurt them or who resemble those who have hurt them.

The most secret of all hurt-backs is *hidden self-destruction*. Families may not notice that one of their members is on a self-destructive path until the destruction has reached a crisis stage. Explicit pattern addictions—with more obvious cords such as eating disorders and nicotine and drug addiction—are often the signals of this complex cording. And here again, the family member identified as having the "problem" may be neither the source of the problem, nor the one actually having the problem, but rather the one acting the problem out for someone else.

Lower-Level Love Forms Cords

We have looked briefly at lies, confusion and pain in terms of cording. However, not all cording is attributable to negative or undesirable emotion. Friendship forms cords. Sexual pleasure forms cords. Interpersonal love forms cords, cords between people's emotional bodies and also between their physical bodies.

Recall the discussion of unconditional, high, pure love in chapter 9. This love is cord-free in that it is unconditional and unattached to any particular person, place or thing. Conditions imposed by lower-level, emotional love are cords. Emotional love, no matter how beautiful, is attachment-based.

Exercise 18.1: Clearing a Heart Cord

Remember that this is only an exercise and you can decide not to take the results of this exercise back to what you call "real life."

Choose someone you love or have loved. Close your eyes. See this person in front of you, facing you. Visualize a cord or string running from that person's heart to your heart. See how this cord attaches to each of your hearts as if it had roots like a tree growing into these hearts. Feel the effects of this glowing but cloudy-colored cord and its roots on your heart for a while. . . .

Then turn this cord, which is now of a cloudy light, to a very bright white light. See this cord vaporize. Say, "Release me. I release you."

Exercise 18.2: Clearing a Point Cord

Repeat the above exercise, this time shifting from the heart to other points in the two participating bodies, such as the stomach or the genitals or the forehead.

Exercise 18.3: Clearing the Social Energy Web

Repeat the above exercises, this time involving several persons in your life and cords between several points on your body and theirs. Visualize and construct an elaborate web. Feel the points where the cords attach and root. Then light up all the cords you see and vaporize them. Light up. Deconstruct. Transmute to the highest light.

Feel the sensation following the transmutation to high light. Now decide whether or not to reinstate the cords you just vaporized. Watch yourself decide and watch yourself act upon this decision.

Chapter 19

Letting Go

It is for the sake of the body that time and place and physical movement exist; for bodies could not be constructed if there were no place for them, and bodies could not change if there were not time and physical movement.

—Hermes to Ammon,

Hermetica

Just seeing, perceiving webs and all of the cords with which they are woven is a great accomplishment. You can be certain that you will use this ability in all of your current and future activities and interactions. Death, whether it be an "in life" death, physical death or another profound transition, is a very demanding task. Once you have learned to see the cords that attach to this world, you still have more to do. Once you can see the cords, *you must learn to let them go. A successful transition requires letting go of cords that may impede that transition.*

Even when an individual believes she or he has released all attachments, the clearing of the cords is not necessarily entirely completed. Oftentimes, the basic clearing does not complete—it resists a full letting go. Some degree of hanging on continues, usually unconsciously. Somehow the release does not allow a full letting go.

There are several reasons for this resistance or inability to let go. One is that it takes energy to let go, especially when the cord being let go is a strong two-way cord. This situation is common to many love relationships in which, even when wanting to "break up," neither member really lets go. Sometimes lovers take turns letting go and hanging on. A full letting go is never achieved this way. Even when all players involved feel they have released all attachments, they may hang on.

Use Paradox for Energy

Energy helps the letting go. Here paradox can be used to gather energy to fuel full release. Recall the discussion of paradox in Volume One of this series and also the depiction of paradox in this volume's Figure 6.2. See that paradox serves a purpose. Without the intensity of the tension, the feeling of being trapped in an energy-binding situation, there may be insufficient or no energy, desire or impetus for release, for moving on, for breaking free.

The tension created by paradoxes, when used well, can generate enough energy to break out of these paradoxes. In this sense, *the paradox always contains the energy for its own solution.* You will remember this when you most need to know it. Without the painful tenseness of paradox, we cannot experience the full release—the jump or shift in perception, the total letting go—that is produced by breaking out of the rigid web of the paradoxical double bind.

We must learn to spot paradoxes before they stagnate in order to harvest the valuable energy produced at their peak. There are three parts to this essential awareness:

- Detect the paradox.
- Feel the energy trapped within the paradox.
- Release yourself from the paradox at its peak to take the most energy away with you.

Exercise 19.1: Using Paradox to Fuel Letting Go

Clear some space around you. Extend your arms outward, reaching horizontally away from your shoulders. Hold this position and close your eyes.

Imagine that there is a person on either side of you holding on to your hand and pulling on it in the direction reaching away from your body. Feel these people pulling on you harder and harder. Feel as if you are being pulled in half.

Feel as if you are trapped in this intense tugging on you in opposite directions. Trapped. Feel also as if you have tied these pulls to you, that as uncomfortable as these pulls are, you engaged or participated in setting up this situation.

Begin to struggle fiercely for a release. Struggle with no success for a while. As you struggle, feel that your arms are being pulled even harder in opposite directions. Struggle. Struggle. Struggle.

Suddenly, there is a letting go.

That's it.

Let go, and you will be free. Refine your ability to harvest energy from paradox. The release of this energy, of *your* energy, is a death. This is a death release. Use the energy you free up, the energy you release, to fully break the cords, the holds on you that have been obstructing the clean and healthy death of your life situation.

Fine-Tune the Release

Understanding and applying the use of paradox in kicking off a full transition is important. Once you sensitize yourself to this process, you can fine-tune the release you generate. In other words, *releasing energy to fuel a complete letting go* is great. However, there is more to do. Direct this wonderfully released energy; fine-tune this release. Use the energy you release to empower the process, to direct the energy in a constructive direction, to raise the level and purity of energy you have to transform.

Exercise 19.2: Focusing the Release

Imagine that you are a balloon about to burst. Someone or something is continuing to pump air into you. The pressure mounts. Take a deep breath; expand your lungs and abdomen. Open your eyeballs very wide. Fill your cheeks with more air than they seem to be able to hold. Hold this expansion a moment.

While you hold, imagine that when you let out all this air, you will release your essence with it. Continue to hold this expansion—still hold your breath. Choose a place your essence will go, and also choose a degree of light that your essence will take on when you release it. When you release yourself, you will go to this place and become this light. Hold. Prepare to burst.

Now burst, go there and become light.

Chapter 20

Avoiding
Primary Reconnection

From here on go out and calculate
that which the mouth cannot speak
and the ear cannot hear.
—Sefer Yetzirah 4:16

Now you have detected the networks of cords (the patterns and definitions of your reality to which you have grown addicted), the world with which you have surrounded yourself, which others have connected to you. After you have released those cords, those attachments—the obvious attachments as well as the subtle energy attachments and the subtle and obvious social energy attachments—after you have truly let go of all your attachment to your self (your physical, social, emotional and other levels of self), there is something more you must do. *You must avoid primary reconnection.* In order to avoid primary reconnection, you must be aware of not only what reconnection looks like but how the first reconnection feels. You will remember the information offered here at the times you need it.

See Reconnection Forming

It may seem premature to have to concern yourself with the problem of reconnection so soon after you begin to manage detachment, release and full letting go. However, the tempo of dying requires your immediate sensitivity to the matters of incidental and purposeful reconnection. You *can* be ready to deal with reconnection as soon as it begins. You already have the necessary awareness and alertness.

You *can* see, with your inner eye, the many networks of cords, the overall web you weave. You can see each of the bits, the pieces of energy, out of which each cord is formed. This acuity of inner vision comes with concentration and with the giving of permission to your imagination to lead the way. "Fake it till you make it" takes on new meaning here.

Similarly, you can detect even the first hints of the reconnection process. You can see the first bits of energy you collect around the attachment points. You can see the early signs of recording. Once you use your inner eye to see this, you know. If your inner eye is still closed, you can manage to know by being alert to subtle sensations that alert you to the hooking in of cords seeking reestablishment.

Note Key Reconnect Hooks

Reconnection can occur before you leave your physical body as well as after. Living deaths such as divorces, job terminations and major moves are prime targets for reconnection. While you are still in your physical body, the spots that have been de-corded may hunger for the attachments that have been lost. If the spots have not been sealed, they are like vacuums sucking in similar or the same hooks. Sealing the door to reconnection is not possible when a full, clean release has not been accomplished.

There are points on the physical body most likely to be hooked to old cords again. These are the heart, the throat, the solar plexus, the lower abdomen and the genital area. There are also points on the emotional body most likely to hook old cords. These are points through which old emotional cords traveled and sucked in emotional energy. These are special points in the emotional body to be very aware of, because they are points where the cords of others were once deeply rooted or are still attached.

Living endings and deaths such as graduation, divorce, job loss and identity crisis are preliminary deaths. They are exercises in detaching, transitioning and moving on. These deaths offer lessons that can be learned if we are able to see the point. Preliminary death is practice for physical death.

Keep in mind that physical death has several stages prior to, during and following the so-called medical death of the body (as discussed in Volume One). In short, we might say here that the actual physical-body death is one of the first stages of physical death. The process of detaching from the body also involves an emotional death, a second stage of physical death. Those who do not recognize that one must continue to release cords throughout this second stage of death (emotional death) may enter it bewildered and confused—or even hysterical, fearful or angry— and needlessly spend their precious spiritual energy. *They may waste their spiritual energy struggling in the remains of the web woven during life, releasing some cords but hungering to reconnect some released cords.*

Whether it be a preliminary emotional death, such as divorce, or the more complete physical-/emotional-body death, you may find yourself in such a morass of confused energy. When you do, focus on the chant:

- light up
- deconstruct
- transmute to the higher light.*

Any faint hint of reconnection must be immediately addressed this way. Focus on the initial re-rooting. Then light up, deconstruct and transmute to the highest light.

The third stage of physical death is mental-body death. There are also points of potential connection and reconnection on the mental body. Because the mental body is amorphous, these points are vague. Think more in terms of density of energy. Where the energy knots or is somewhat thicker or denser in the mental body, a cord can re-root.

Hold to Your Intent

You are not the only cause of reconnection. So many beings and energies from your old life seek to stay corded with you. Once you have decided to move on, to transit out of your old life or body, you may be pulled back by the longings of others. Regardless of your perceptions of the intentions of those who seek to reconnect or remain connected, even in the face of your profound release of all attachment, you must *hold to your intent.* If your intent is to die out of your old life, vigilantly dissolve all attempts at reconnection. You can reestablish communication of a higher, purer detached form later, after you have succeeded in dying. (If you truly master

---

* As noted earlier, forms of this process are found in numerous spiritual teachings of diverse origin. Here, this form is reframed for the practice of release, specifically death- and transition-related release of one's own and others' attachments to one's life.

this process, you may be able to transform these connections while in the process of dying. Otherwise, wait until your death is complete.)

Exercise 20.1: Detecting Reconnection

Visualize yourself sitting across from someone you do not know at all. Tell yourself that even though you do not know this person, you did once know this person, you just have no ready memory of him or her. Now visualize this person attempting to form an attachment to you.

See the pieces of a cord extending toward you from its roots in the heart, solar plexus, stomach area, groin, forehead, throat or whatever location you choose of that person whom you do not know. Forming its growth in the air, the cord grows from that person in your direction, toward you, becoming a longer and longer and stronger and stronger cord. As it nears you, you begin to feel the roots of the cord reaching ahead of itself trying to root in you.

See clearly where that cord seeks to attach to you.

Exercise 20.2: Avoiding and Deterring the Re-Cordings of Others

Return to where you were when you ended the previous exercise (Exercise 20.1). The cord approaches you, seeking to reconnect.

Create an invisible but very thick force field through which that cord cannot penetrate. See that cord trying to penetrate, finding ways around the shield, and see that you beat the cord at every corner, at every attempt, with your perfect shield, not allowing that cord in, no matter how valiant its efforts. Close your eyes and feel entirely encased in your own self-designed protective shield. Hold for the next exercise.

Exercise 20.3: Transmuting Reconnecting Cords to Light

You are safe behind your shield. Scan your consciousness for any thought of cording to the person you face. If you see even the slightest bit of this taking place, take action: light up, deconstruct and transmute what you see or imagine to be any bits of forming cords. Catch these forming cords as early as possible—in the space between your consciousness and the consciousness connected to the other end of these cords.

Chapter 21

LEAP Level Three: Willing the Exit from the Flesh

A season is set for everything, a time for every experience under heaven: A time for being born and a time for dying . . .
—Ecclesiastes 3,
TANAKH: THE HOLY SCRIPTURES

Once you know that it is time for you to die, hanging on to your old attachments renders you not yourself but instead a deteriorating museum of yourself. You must now let go to live, release for your consciousness to indeed survive.

The words in this volume encourage you to develop your sense of consciousness. They encourage you to feel when it is time for you to embrace your transitions and deaths. They encourage you to detect energy, cords and webs. They also encourage you to see the light. They moreover ask you to turn your eye toward the beyond.

What is the beyond? The beyond is simply a place where your energy can be free of the detrimental patterns, the rigid energy formations trapping it. The beyond is simply beyond where you are now.

LEAP Out

We have explained how just *wanting* to release attachments and cords may not fuel the exit from the body or from the lifestyle you have been wearing. What is required is a great LEAP out. Understanding the nature of the LEAP is something you must do on all levels of your existence.

Essential in making the LEAP out of the flesh of one's old life is the will to make this LEAP. Again, the use of will is relevant to this examination of death. Rarely, when busy living a life, does one think about mustering up the will to leave that life. And when this thought does surface, it may be classified as crazy, destructive or suicidal. However, the will to exit a particular life need not be hysterical or emotional or suicidal. It can be quite practical. At a particular time in any death process, the effectiveness of the process is enhanced by the injection of energy produced by the will. *Being sensitive to the presence of will is the first step in its application.*

Will the Exit

What does it mean to will the exit? To apply one's will this way is to focus the will in such a concentrated way that the exit from the phase of life or physical body is facilitated. *Strength of will* certainly empowers the exit, and this strength is garnered with exercise and practice. If, however, you feel that you do not have time to build up your will before you undergo a death, you can rely on *clarity of will.*

With a clear intent to exit, the passage is eased regardless of the strength the will has accumulated over time. This is a basic principle of consciousness technology. Clarity *is* strength—and concurrently clarity is the most immediate entry into strength. Think of a very strong, heavy pair of scissors. The scissors may be strong and heavy enough not to break when cutting something thick. Think of the sharpness of the scissors as clarity. A very sharp pair of scissors cuts through heavy material as well as or better than strong but dull scissors. The sharp scissors were sharpened with the clear intent to cut well. Your will can be this sharp by declaring your intent to be this sharp.

Exercise 21.1: Finding the Will

We have talked again and again about the use of will and the nature of one's will. Now you will feel for yourself your own will.

Begin to look for your will. Will that you find your will. How does willing feel? You are isolating the essence of your will. This exercise generates a refinement of your will by asking you to locate your will. Seeking the will refines it.

Close your eyes, go inside and take some time to find your will. Realize that your will is not your relationship to the outside world, not your list of responsibilities, not your set of accomplishments . . . not your failures, not your feelings, not your attachments or cords, not your family, not your political party, not your philosophical beliefs, not your religion.

Now you are locating your will, the force manifested by the essence of your consciousness. Once you have found your will or what you sense is your will, continue refining your connection to your will. Feel as if you are getting to better know your will.

Hold your concentration on your will for the next exercise. As

---

you hold, get to know better what "will" really is. Define your will for yourself.

Exercise 21.2: Willing the Exit

Take your will into your forehead. Now move your will to the center of the top of your head.

Now, as if you are pushing on something very hard with all your will, push your self out the top of your head—will yourself out of your body.

Hold your will outside your body, above your head, for a while.

Now focus on this will of yours—the will you have come to recognize. Move this will back down to the top of your head. Pull your will back into your body through the top of your head.

For now, you remain in your physical body.

Do not mistake will for ego. These are two different functions, and will can be contaminated, even corrupted, by the mixing of the two.

EPILOGUE

Living the Keys to Transition and Death

We tend to think that much of what we do not see is inaccessible to us and that there are mysteries we are not armed to solve. We have somehow become accommodated to a notion that ease of transition and movement in and out of the physical plane—by physical death or other means—is not readily available to us at all times. Somewhere deep in the messages we have historically been provided with is the concept that the keys to the matrix-shifting we need to be able to do consciously (to transit minor and major changes and deaths effectively) are "mysteries."

Yet the keys are everywhere around us and within us. And being able to spot these keys is our birthright. The only mystery may be suppression of this information and the historical treating of this information as something very special to which only a few are entitled.

Let's dispel the mystery concept. Let's release ourselves from limitations that are not our limitations. The simple exercises and discussions in this volume have moved through awarenesses much the way exercising one's physical body on a weight circuit in a gym moves through each muscle group step by step until the entire physical body has been exercised. In so doing, three levels of the light-energy-action process have been tapped. We have signaled ourselves that it is time to know these levels of travel and change: embracing, quickening and willing the exit.

Seeing Cycles	Ground Level of LEAPs	Volume One
One	Embracing	Volume Two
Two	Quickening	Volume Two
Three	Willing the Exit	Volume Two

Now follow on into Volumes Three and Four of this *Continuity of Life* series to share in this great adventure of transition, transformation and death. Now that the foundation for this form of thinking has been laid, we can LEAP beyond it into realms to which we have every right to travel.

Take the keys, ride these LEAPs and know that contrary to what you may have been taught . . .

THE LIFE FORCE DOES NOT DIE.

YOU DO NOT DIE.

List of Exercises

About the Author

Author, lecturer, psychotherapist and social scientist Dr. Angela deAngelis earned her two doctorates and two masters degrees at the University of California Berkeley, where she lectured in three departments for over a decade. Angela has served as a U.S. National Institute of Mental Health Postdoctoral Fellow; a U.S. Administration on Children, Youth and Families Fellow; and a U.S. Public Health Department Fellow. She has taught, researched, designed and implemented programs in several fields key to this work on the ongoing nature of the life force, among these being: loss and grief; adult, teen and child development; family violence; substance and behavioral addiction; and mental health. Over the past three decades, she has also worked directly in organizational, clinical, educational and faith settings, with several thousand persons experiencing emotional, substance, relationship and behavioral addictions and "co"-addictions, and other relationship challenges, as well as stress, anxiety and other "disorders." She has also worked with the children of many of the above. Dr. deAngelis is director of the Metaxis Institute based in Corte Madera, California.

Continuity of Life
Seminars and Consultations
by
Dr. Angela deAngelis

Change your life. Change your transitions. Reach beyond unnecessary limits.

Empower yourself to address the large and small challenges, transitions and crises of life—including but not limited to problematic addictions, troubled relationships, difficult and chronic mental and physical health conditions, grief and loss, and death and dying.

Dr. Angela deAngelis is available for consults, treatment programs, workshops, seminars, retreats and trainings. To make appointments and reservations, and to be placed on the Continuity of Life mailing list, email your contact information (including telephone, email address and postal mailing address) to:

DoctorAngela@aol.com
MetaxisInstitute@aol.com

Also check the following websites for information on upcoming events:

DoctorAngela.com
MetaxisInstitute.com

TRANSITION AND SURVIVAL TECHNOLOGIES:
Inter-Dimensional Consciousness As Healing, Survival and Beyond

by Dr. Angela deAngelis

Take a new look at healing, health, life, daily challenges and transitions, even death. "Transition and Survival Technologies" takes readers further on an inner and inter-dimensional journey into the worlds of healing, transitioning, shifting realities, dying — into the worlds the human consciousness has a right to and can indeed access to heal and survive here and beyond.

TRANSITION AND SURVIVAL TECHNOLOGIES $16.95
Softcover, 224pp, ISBN-13: 978-1-891824-68-5

We can free our attention to focus upon something much more subtle, abstract and more real than our so-called "worldly" experiences. Once we are fully liberated and our perceptions set free to see, a new kind of understanding or vision of reality can come to us. We can then see ourselves as something far more – far greater – than we believed ourselves to be.

Chapters Include

- **Leaving the Body**
- **Releasing the Old Matrix: Energetic**
- **Shedding**
- **Dissolving the Self: At the Membrane**
- **Rebundling: Dance of (Re)Creation**
- **Reformatting the Self: Free of Cords**
- **Delivering Oneself into Another Dimension**
- **Merging—But with What?**

- **Discerning What Beckons**
- **Knowing the Escorts**
- **Protecting the Self in the Eyes of Interdimensional Law**
- **Shedding and Dying with Purpose**
- **Understanding How Many Behaviors Are Suiciding**
- **Healing as Living Ascension into New Energetic Patterns**

ORDER ONLINE AT WWW.LIGHTTECHNOLOGY.COM
Phone: 928-526-1345 • 800-450-0985 • Fax: 928-714-1132
customersrv@lighttechnology.net

HEALING EARTH IN ALL HER DIMENSIONS:
Personal, Species, and Planetary Healing
by Dr. Angela deAngelis

HEALING EARTH IN ALL HER DIMENSIONS $16.95
Softcover, 224pp, ISBN-13: 978-1-891824-69-2

Explore how interdimensional shifts can be applied to help heal individual bodies, as well as global and ecological systems, to bring about the healing and survival of yourself and the entire human species.

Gain confidence in the truly enduring nature of your consciousness and come to understand how powerful your conscious will, your free will, truly is. With knowledge comes the realization that you can access this eternal and powerful nature before leaving (or traveling to and from) your physical body.

Expand your ability to independently evolve from your physical body. Prepare the way to expand beyond unnecessary limitations to develop new patterns of existence, healing and transition for yourself, your species and your ecosystem.

Chapters Include

- How to Metamorph
- Living the Metamorphosis
- Conscious Healing
- Conscious Shift Construction
- Conscious Metamorphosis
- Breaking Addictions to Perceived Reality
- Meta-somatic Ailments
- Metascending to a New Niche: LEAP Level Seven
- Entering Metaterra: How to Access High Metaxis
- Conquering Catastrophe Completely
- Becoming the Phoenix and Rising
- Fueling Freely Willed Ascension
- Dying with Grace and Power

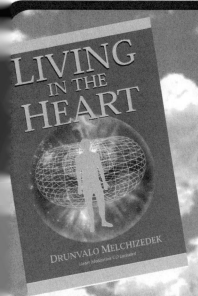

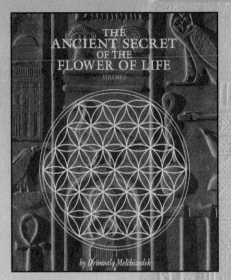

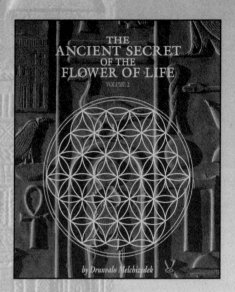

Light Technology

Enjoy All of these Great Books

Sedona: Sacred Earth
Nicholas R. Mann

This book is an attempt to describe the power of Sedona. I bring in native traditions, geology, geometry and physics to try and explain what makes Sedona so special, what makes it so memorable. Yet, although you may be an anthropologist, a geologist, a mathematician or a physicist, you don't have to be one to grasp what is in this book!

$14.95 Softcover, 147 p. ISBN: 1-891824-45-7

Pathways and Parables for a Changing World
Miriandra Rota

Here we are! We know this is a powerful time; we have successfully birthed ourselves to be present during the grand awakening. We can feel it—the call to powerful living! This book is about practical solutions called pathways. Have you ever asked Pretty Flower a question only to have her answer begin with, "Once upon a time . . ."?

$19.95 Softcover, 380 p. ISBN: 1-891824-53-8

The Gentle Way
Tom T. Moore

This self-help book will put you back in touch with your guardian angels or strengthen your spiritual beliefs. You will have more fun and less stress in your life. It will assist you in achieving whatever goals you have set for yourself in your life. It will assist you in handling those major challenges we all experience in life. This book is for people of all faiths and beliefs—the only requirement is a basic belief in angels.

$14.95 Softcover, 140 p. ISBN: 1-891824-60-0

Shining the Light
Book VII
Robert Shapiro

Now, many of you have been reading this series of *Shining the Light* books for some time and so you are reasonably well informed about the circumstances in the U.S. and in the world regarding who is doing what to whom—at least in an overall sense, without naming names too much. The objective is to move through—not jump over, but move through—the impossible to solutions that have no logical means to explain them.

$24.95 Softcover, 521 p. ISBN: 1-891824-55-4

This School Called Planet Earth
Summer Bacon

In her channelings, Summer Bacon has proven herself as one of the clearest and most authentic trance mediums today. Dr. Peebles, through Summer Bacon, has shown us that humor can go with enlightenment. With chapters teaching us ways of embodying energy, collecting wisdom, creating intimacy with all life and more, they have created a work that will stick with you on your voyage to the discovery of the self.

$16.95 Softcover, 323 pgs. ISBN: 1-891824-54-6

Ascension Series:
How to be Financially Successful • Book 15
Dr. Joshua Stone

As one of the most successful businessmen of the New Age movement, Dr. Stone has written an easily digestible book full of tools and advice for achieving prosperity. This book conveys esoteric secrets of the universe. It will change not only your finances, but your life.

$14.95 Softcover, 236 p. ISBN: 1-891824-55-4

Phone: 928-526-1345 or 1-800-450-0985 • Fax: 928-714-1132

Publishing Presents

Plus Hundreds More!

A New Formula For Creation
Judith Moore

This book brings an inspiring positive message regarding the future of our planet. Earth is experiencing the Shift of the Ages, a time marked by massive Earth changes and social upheaval. This is foretold in many prophecies, including Hopi prophecies and the biblical Revelations. They warn that raising consciousness is the only way to avert a massive cataclysm.

$16.95 Softcover, 186 p. ISBN: 1-891824-57-0

Living in the Heart
(With CD)
Drunvalo Melchizedek

This is a book of remembering. You have always had this place within your heart, and it is still there now. It existed before creation, and it will exist even after the last star shines its brilliant light. This book is written with the least amount of words possible to convey the meaning and to keep the integrity of the essence of this experience. The images are purposefully simple. It is written from the heart, not the mind.

$25.00 Softcover, 120 p. ISBN: 1-891824-43-0

Ancient Secret of the Flower of Life *Vol. I*
Drunvalo Melchizedek

Once, all life in the universe knew the Flower of Life as the creation pattern —the geometrical design leading us into and out of physical existence. Sacred Geometry is the form beneath our being and points to a divine order in our reality. We can follow that order from the invisible atom to the infinite stars, finding ourselves at each step.

$25.00 Softcover, 228 p. ISBN: 1-891824-17-1

Change Your Encodements, Your DNA, Your Life!
Amma through Cathy Chapman

The first part of this book discusses what you call love. Love is the most powerful energy. The second part contains powerful techniques for working with your DNA encodements. The third part contains what some call predictions, which are nothing more than my reading and interpretation of the energy at the time when the energy was read.

$16.95 Softcover, 303 p. ISBN: 1-891824-52-X

Animal Souls Speak
Explorer Race Series
Robert Shapiro

Welcome to the footsteps of the loving beings (animals) who support you, who wish to reveal more about themselves to you and who welcome you, not only to planet Earth, but more specifically to the pathway of self-discovery. The animal world will speak through elders, since that way they can include knowledge and wisdom about their home planets. Each animal brings a wonderous gift to share with humanity—enjoy it!

$29.95 Softcover, 610 p. ISBN: 1-891824-50-3

Ancient Secret of the Flower of Life *Vol. II*
Drunvalo Melchizedek

Drunvalo shares the instructions for the Mer-Ka-Ba meditation, step-by-step techniques for the re-creation of the energy field of the evolved human. From the pyramids and mysteries of Egypt to the new race of Indigo children, Drunvalo presents the sacred geometries of the Reality and the subtle energies that shape our world.

$25.00 Softcover, 477 p. ISBN: 1-891824-21-X

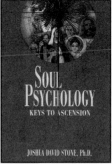

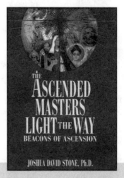

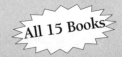

THE EXPLORER RACE SERIES

ZOOSH AND HIS FRIENDS THROUGH ROBERT SHAPIRO

THE SERIES: Humans—creators-in-training—have a purpose and destiny so heartwarmingly, profoundly glorious that it is almost unbelievable from our present dimensional perspective. Humans are great lightbeings from beyond this creation, gaining experience in dense physicality. This truth about the great human genetic experiment of the Explorer Race and the mechanics of creation is being revealed for the first time by Zoosh and his friends through superchannel Robert Shapiro. These books read like adventure stories as we follow the clues from this creation that we live in out to the Council of Creators and beyond.

❶ THE EXPLORER RACE

You individuals reading this are truly a result of the genetic experiment on Earth. You are beings who uphold the principles of the Explorer Race. The information in this book is designed to show you who you are and give you an evolutionary understanding of your past that will help you now. The key to empowerment in these days is to not know everything about your past, but to know what will help you now. Your number-one function right now is your status of Creator apprentice, which you have achieved through years and lifetimes of sweat. You are constantly being given responsibilities by the Creator that would normally be things that Creator would do. The responsibility and the destiny of the Explorer Race is not only to explore, but to create. 574 P. $25.00 ISBN 0-929385-38-1

❷ ETs and the EXPLORER RACE

In this book, Robert channels Joopah, a Zeta Reticulan now in the ninth dimension who continues the story of the great experiment—the Explorer Race—from the perspective of his civilization. The Zetas would have been humanity's future selves had not humanity re-created the past and changed the future. 237 P. $14.95 ISBN 0-929385-79-9

❸ EXPLORER RACE: ORIGINS and the NEXT 50 YEARS

This volume has so much information about who we are and where we came from—the source of male and female beings, the war of the sexes, the beginning of the linear mind, feelings, the origin of souls—it is a treasure trove. In addition, there is a section that relates to our near future—how the rise of global corporations and politics affects our future, how to use benevolent magic as a force of creation and how we will go out to the stars and affect other civilizations. Astounding information. 339 P. $14.95 ISBN 0-929385-95-0

❹ EXPLORER RACE: CREATORS and FRIENDS
The MECHANICS of CREATION

Now that you have a greater understanding of who you are in the larger sense, it is necessary to remind you of where you came from, the true magnificence of your being. You must understand that you are creators-in-training, and yet you were once a portion of Creator. One could certainly say, without being magnanimous, that you are still a portion of Creator, yet you are training for the individual responsibility of being a creator, to give your Creator a coffee break. This book will allow you to understand the vaster qualities and help you remember the nature of the desires that drive any creator, the responsibilities to which a creator must answer, the reaction a creator must have to consequences and the ultimate reward of any creator. 435 P. $19.95 ISBN 1-891824-01-5

❺ EXPLORER RACE: PARTICLE PERSONALITIES

All around you in every moment you are surrounded by the most magical and mystical beings. They are too small for you to see as single individuals, but in groups you know them as the physical matter of your daily life. Particles who might be considered either atoms or portions of atoms consciously view the vast spectrum of reality yet also have a sense of personal memory like your own linear memory. These particles remember where they have been and what they have done in their infinitely long lives. Some of the particles we hear from are Gold, Mountain Lion, Liquid Light, Uranium, the Great Pyramid's Capstone, This Orb's Boundary, Ice and Ninth-Dimensional Fire. 237 P. $14.95 ISBN 0-929385-97-7

❻ EXPLORER RACE and BEYOND

With a better idea of how creation works, we go back to the Creator's advisers and receive deeper and more profound explanations of the roots of the Explorer Race. The liquid Domain and the Double Diamond portal share lessons given to the roots on their way to meet the Creator of this universe, and finally the roots speak of their origins and their incomprehensibly long journey here. 360 P. $14.95 ISBN 1-891824-06-6

THE EXPLORER RACE SERIES

ZOOSH AND HIS FRIENDS THROUGH ROBERT SHAPIRO

⑦ EXPLORER RACE: The COUNCIL of CREATORS

The thirteen core members of the Council of Creators discuss their adventures in coming to awareness of themselves and their journeys on the way to the Council on this level. They discuss the advice and oversight they offer to all creators, including the Creator of this local universe. These beings are wise, witty and joyous, and their stories of Love's Creation create an expansion of our concepts as we realize that we live in an expanded, multiple-level reality. 237 P. $14.95 ISBN 1-891824-13-9

⑧ EXPLORER RACE and ISIS

This is an amazing book! It has priestess training, Shamanic training, Isis's adventures with Explorer Race beings—before Earth and on Earth—and an incredibly expanded explanation of the dynamics of the Explorer Race. Isis is the prototypal loving, nurturing, guiding feminine being, the focus of feminine energy. She has the ability to expand limited thinking without making people with limited beliefs feel uncomfortable. She is a fantastic storyteller, and all of her stories are teaching stories. If you care about who you are, why you are here, where you are going and what life is all about—pick up this book. You won't lay it down until you are through, and then you will want more. 317 P. $14.95 ISBN 1-891824-11-2

⑨ EXPLORER RACE and JESUS

The core personality of that being known on the Earth as Jesus, along with his students and friends, describes with clarity and love his life and teaching two thousand years ago. He states that his teaching is for all people of all races in all countries. Jesus announces here for the first time that he and two others, Buddha and Mohammed, will return to Earth from their place of being in the near future, and a fourth being, a child already born now on Earth, will become a teacher and prepare humanity for their return. So heartwarming and interesting, you won't want to put it down. 354 P. $16.95 ISBN 1-891824-14-7

⑩ EXPLORER RACE: Earth History and Lost Civilization

Speaks of Many Truths and Zoosh, through Robert Shapiro, explain that planet Earth, the only water planet in this solar system, is on loan from Sirius as a home and school for humanity, the Explorer Race. Earth's recorded history goes back only a few thousand years, its archaeological history a few thousand more. Now this book opens up as if a light was on in the darkness, and we see the incredible panorama of brave souls coming from other planets to settle on different parts of Earth. We watch the origins of tribal groups and the rise and fall of civilizations, and we can begin to understand the source of the wondrous diversity of plants, animals and humans that we enjoy here on beautiful Mother Earth. 310 P. $14.95 ISBN 1-891824-20-1

⑪ EXPLORER RACE: ET VISITORS SPEAK

Even as you are searching the sky for extraterrestrials and their spaceships, ETs are here on planet Earth—they are stranded, visiting, exploring, studying the culture, healing the Earth of trauma brought on by irresponsible mining or researching the history of Christianity over the past two thousand years. Some are in human guise, and some are in spirit form. Some look like what we call animals as they come from the species' home planet and interact with their fellow beings—those beings that we have labeled cats or cows or elephants. Some are brilliant cosmic mathematicians with a sense of humor; they are presently living here as penguins. Some are fledgling diplomats training for future postings on Earth when we have ET embassies here. In this book, these fascinating beings share their thoughts, origins and purposes for being here. 350 P. $14.95 ISBN 1-891824-28-7

⑫ EXPLORER RACE: Techniques for GENERATING SAFETY

Wouldn't you like to generate safety so you could go wherever you need to go and do whatever you need to do in a benevolent, safe and loving way for yourself? Learn safety as a radiated environment that will allow you to gently take the step into the new timeline, into a benevolent future and away from a negative past. 208 P. $9.95 ISBN 1-891824-26-0

Phone: 928-526-1345 or 1-800-450-0985 • Fax 928-714-1132

... or use our online bookstore at www.lighttechnology.com